Nick Vandome

Mac OS X Leopard

in easy steps

In easy steps is an imprint of In Easy Steps Limited
Southfield Road · Southam
Warwickshire CV47 0FB · United Kingdom
www.ineasysteps.com

Notice of Liability
Every effort has been made to ensure that this book contains accurate
and current information. However, In Easy Steps Limited and the
author shall not be liable for any loss or damage suffered by readers
as a result of any information contained herein.

Trademarks
Mac OS X® is a registered trademark of Apple Computer, Inc. All
other trademarks are acknowledged as belonging to their respective
companies.

Printed and bound in the United Kingdom

ISBN-13 978-1-84078-350-6
ISBN-10 1-84078-350-8

Contents

1 Introducing Leopard

OS X Leopard is the latest operating system from Apple Computers. It is promoted as being easy and enjoyable to use and also very stable for a computer operating system. This chapter introduces the OS X interface and shows how to get started with it.

About OS X

In 1984 Apple Computers introduced a new operating system (OS) for its Macintosh computers and, at the time, it was revolutionary. Instead of having to access programs and files through lines of lengthy computer code commands, users could navigate their way through Apple computers using a new Graphical User Interface (GUI). This produced the same results as the previous method, but it was much easier for the user: instead of having to type in lines of computer coding it was possible to access files and programs by clicking on buttons, icons and drop down menus. This ease of use was a major factor in the mass adoption of personal computers and this type of operating system soon began to appear on all personal computers, not just Macs.

Over the years Apple refined its OS and added more and more functions with each new release. However, like any operating system the Mac OS was not without its problems: it was as prone to crashes as any other operating system and it had its own quirky idiosyncrasies, such as extension conflicts (when two programs refused to cohabit on the same machine).

When Apple decided to upgrade their OS from version 9 they were faced with two choices: add more code to what was becoming an incredibly complicated structure for the Apple programmers to work with, or, create an entirely new program from scratch. Thankfully, they chose the second option, and the result is OS X (pronounced "ten").

In some ways OS X is a contradiction of Apple's original philosophy: while it retains and enhances its traditional ease of use, it is also based on the UNIX programming language, the very type of thing that Apple was trying to get away from in 1984. The reason it is based on UNIX is that this is a very stable operating environment and ensures that OS X is one of the most stable consumer operating systems that has ever been designed. However, for most users, they can be blissfully unaware of the very existence of UNIX if they want and just enjoy its benefits while using the new Aqua interface of OS X and all of the advantages that this brings. For the programming expert, there is also an option of delving into UNIX itself and getting to grips with this side of the program. Leopard is the fifth version of OS X and one of the most advanced operating system seen to date.

Don't forget

UNIX is an operating system that has traditionally been used for large commercial mainframe computers. It is renowned for its stability and ability to be used within different computing environments.

Installing OS X

The first step to install OS X is to insert the CD-ROM into the CD drive. The disk should run automatically and the installation can then proceed as follows:

Don't forget

Make sure you read any of the online documentation before you install OS X. These documents, which are usually in PDF format, can contain useful general information and also any late news about the program that was released after it was produced.

1. Double-click on the Install Mac OS X icon to begin the installation process

2. Click on the Restart button

Don't forget

The registration process consists of entering a few details and then moving through a series of dialog windows. In most cases all you have to do is accept the default settings.

3. Enter your username and password. Click on the OK button. Your computer will then shut down and start up again and take you through the rest of the registration process. This consists of an easy-to-follow wizard

The OS X environment

The first most noticeable element about OS X is its elegant user interface. This has been designed to create a user friendly graphic overlay to the UNIX operating system at the heart of OS X and it is a combination of rich colors and sharp, original graphics. The main elements that make up the initial OS X environment are:

Apple menu   Menu bar   Windows   Disk icons

10

The Dock   Desktop

The Apple menu is standardized throughout OS X, regardless of the program in use

Aqua interface

The name given by Apple to its OS X interface is Aqua. This describes the graphical appearance of the operating system. Essentially, it is just the cosmetic appearance of the elements within the operating system, but they combine to give OS X a rich visual look and feel. Some of the main elements of the Aqua interface are:

Menus

Menus in OS X contain commands for the operating system and any relevant programs. If there is an arrow next to a command it means there are subsequent options for the item:

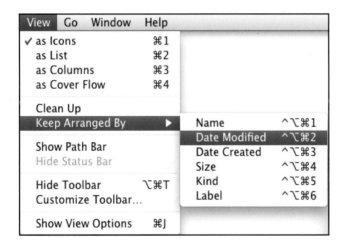

Window buttons

These appear in any open OS X window and can be used to manipulate the window.

Option buttons

Whenever a dialog box with separate options is accessed, OS X highlights the suggested option with a pulsing blue button. This can be accepted by clicking on it or by pressing Enter. If you do not want to accept this option, click on another button in the dialog box.

Don't forget

The graphics used in OS X are designed in a style known as Quartz. The design of this means that some elements, such as menus, allow the background behind them to show through.

Don't forget

The red window button is used to close a window; the amber one to minimize it and the green one to expand it.

Changing the background

Background imagery is an important way to add your own personal touch to your Mac. (This is the graphical element upon which all other items on your computer sit.) There are a range of background options that can be used. To select your own background:

 Click on this icon in the System Preferences folder

Desktop & Screen Saver

You can select your own photographs as your desktop background, once you have loaded them onto your Mac. To do this, select the Pictures Folder in Step 3, and browse to the photograph you want.

2 Click on the Desktop tab

Desktop

3 Select a location from where you want to select a background

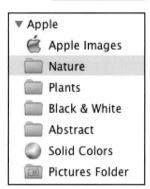

▼ Apple
 Apple Images
 Nature
 Plants
 Black & White
 Abstract
 Solid Colors
 Pictures Folder

4 Click on one of the available backgrounds

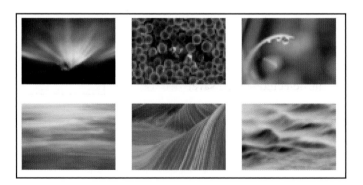

5 The background is applied as the desktop background imagery

Changing the screen saver

A screen saver is the element that appears when the Mac has not been used for a specified period of time. Originally this was designed to avoid screen burn (caused by items being at the same position on the screen for an extended period of time) but now they largely consist of a graphical element. To select your own screen saver:

1 Click on this icon in the System Preferences folder

Desktop &
Screen Saver

Don't forget

Screen savers were originally designed to prevent screen burn (areas of the screen becoming marked as a result of elements remaining static for a prolonged period of time), but now they are more for cosmetic graphical purposes.

2 Click on the Screen Saver tab

Screen Saver

3 Select a location from where you want to select a screen saver

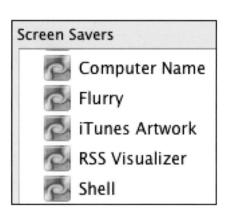

Screen Savers

- Computer Name
- Flurry
- iTunes Artwork
- RSS Visualizer
- Shell

4 Click the Test button to preview the selected screen saver

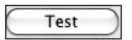

Test

5 Drag this slider to specify the amount of time the Mac is inactive before the screen saver is activated

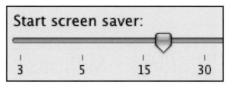

Start screen saver:

3   5   15   30

13

Changing the resolution

For most computer users the size at which items are displayed on the screen is a crucial issue: if items are too small this can make them hard to read and lead to eye strain; too large and you have to spend a lot of time scrolling around to see everything.

The size of items on the screen is controlled by the screen's resolution, i.e. the number of colored dots displayed in an area of the screen. The higher the resolution the smaller the items on the screen, the lower the resolution the larger the items. To change the screen resolution:

Don't forget

A higher resolution makes items appear sharper on the screen, even though they appear physically smaller.

1 Click on this icon in the System Preferences folder

Displays

2 Select a resolution setting to change the overall screen resolution

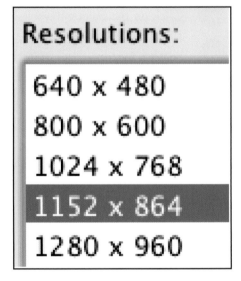

Resolutions:

640 x 480

800 x 600

1024 x 768

1152 x 864

1280 x 960

3 Click here to select the number of colors displayed on the screen (the higher the better)

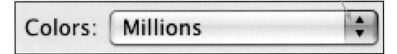

Colors: Millions

Universal Access

In all areas of computing it is important to give as many people access to the system as possible. This includes users with visual impairments and also people who have problems using the mouse and keyboard. In OS X this is achieved through the functions of the Universal Access System Preferences. To use these:

1 Click here once on the Dock to access the System Preferences

2 Click on the Universal Access button

Don't forget

Experiment with the VoiceOver function (in the Seeing window) if only to see how it operates. This will give you a better idea of how visually impaired users access information on a computer.

3 Click on the Seeing tab for help with issues connected with visual impairment

4 Check on the Zoom On button to enable zooming in on specific areas of the screen

5 Check on the White on Black display button to invert the default settings for your system display

...cont'd

6 Click on the Hearing tab to adjust settings for audio problem

Hearing

7 Click on this button to adjust the system volume

Adjust Volume...

8 In the System Preferences click on the Keyboard & Mouse button

Keyboard & Mouse

9 Click on the Mouse tab

Mouse

10 Drag these sliders to change the speed at which the mouse moves and how quickly you have to press it to achieve a double-click operation

Don't forget

Under the Keyboard tab there are options for the time it takes for a keystroke to appear on the screen and how long before a keystroke is repeated if a key is held down for a few seconds.

Background on UNIX

UNIX is the powerful and robust operating system that is the foundation on which OS X runs. In fact, OS X is essentially a very impressive graphical interface placed on top of a version of UNIX known as Darwin.

UNIX was developed in the early 1970s by programmers who wanted to design an operating system that could run on any platform, i.e. different types of computers. Up until then, each operating system had generally been designed for a specific type of computer. Another benefit of UNIX was that it was designed to be available to the whole development community. The program that was used to create UNIX is the now widely used C language.

UNIX first gained popularity in academic institutions and it was then taken on by government organizations. Its adoption by Apple as the foundation for OS X has seen UNIX move into the mainstream of consumer computing. UNIX's greatest strength is its stability, while its greatest weakness is perhaps its non-user-friendliness. Apple have made the most of the former and overcome the latter with its Aqua interface and Quartz graphics.

For people with experience of UNIX, programming can be performed within OS X in the Terminal window. This is the gateway into the UNIX environment and it can be located in Applications>Utilities from the Finder. If you are not familiar with UNIX, you need never worry about it or the Terminal again.

Working with UNIX in the Terminal is not for the uninitiated, or the faint-hearted

Don't forget

In addition to OS X on consumer computers Apple have also released a server that runs on UNIX. This is called XServe and it is used to run and manage computer networks.

17

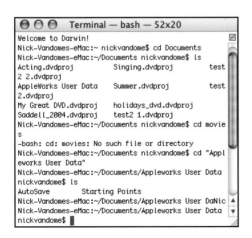

```
Terminal — bash — 52x20
Welcome to Darwin!
Nick-Vandomes-eMac:~ nickvandome$ cd Documents
Nick-Vandomes-eMac:~/Documents nickvandome$ ls
Acting.dvdproj          Singing.dvdproj         test
2 2.dvdproj
AppleWorks User Data    Summer.dvdproj          test
2.dvdproj
My Great DVD.dvdproj    holidays_dvd.dvdproj
Saddell_2004.dvdproj    test2 1.dvdproj
Nick-Vandomes-eMac:~/Documents nickvandome$ cd movie
s
-bash: cd: movies: No such file or directory
Nick-Vandomes-eMac:~/Documents nickvandome$ cd "Appl
eworks User Data"
Nick-Vandomes-eMac:~/Documents/Appleworks User Data
nickvandome$ ls
AutoSave        Starting Points
Nick-Vandomes-eMac:~/Documents/Appleworks User DaNic
Nick-Vandomes-eMac:~/Documents/Appleworks User Data
nickvandome$
```

Shutting down

The Apple menu (which can be accessed by clicking on the Apple icon at the top left corner of the desktop or any subsequent OS X window) has been standardized in OS X. This means that it has the same options regardless of the program in which you are working. This has a number of advantages, not least is the fact that it makes it easier to shut down your Mac. When shutting down, there are three options that can be selected:

- Sleep. This puts the Mac into hibernation mode, i.e. the screen goes blank and the hard drive becomes inactive. This state is maintained until the mouse is moved or a key is pressed on the keyboard. This then wakes up the Mac and it is ready to continue work

- Restart. This closes down the Mac and then restarts it again. This can be useful if you have added new software and your computer requires a restart to make it active

- Shut Down. This closes down the Mac completely once you have finished working

Hot tip

If you install new software you will usually have to restart your Mac before it takes effect.

Don't forget

When shutting down, make sure you have saved all of your open documents, although OS X will prompt you to do this if you have forgotten.

18

Click here to access the Apple menu

Click here to access one of the shut down options

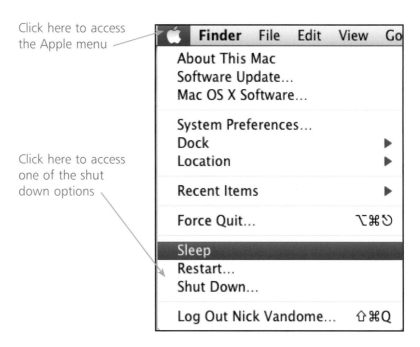

2 Getting up and running

This chapter looks at some of the essential features of OS X. These include the Dock for organizing and accessing all of the elements of the computer, the system preferences for the way the computer looks and operates and items for arranging folders and files.

Introducing the Dock

The Dock is one of the main innovative elements of OS X. Its main function is to help organize and access programs, folders and files. In addition, with its rich translucent colors and elegant graphical icons, it also makes an aesthetically pleasing addition to the desktop. The main things to remember about the Dock are:

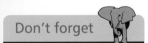
- It is divided into two: programs go on the left of the dividing line; all other items go on the right

- It can be edited in just about any way you choose

By default the Dock appears at the bottom of the screen

20

Programs go here   Dividing line   Open items

Setting Dock preferences

As with most elements of OS X, the Dock can be modified in numerous ways. This can affect both the appearance of the Dock and the way it operates. To set Dock preferences:

1 Select Apple Menu>Dock from the Menu bar

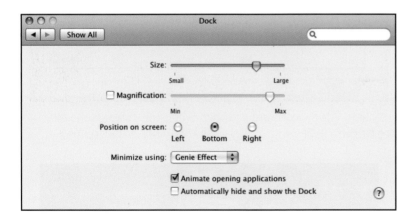

| Turn Hiding On | ⌥⌘D |
| Turn Magnification On | |

Position on Left
✓ Position on Bottom
Position on Right

Dock Preferences...

2 Select the general preferences here

Dock Preferences...

3 Click here to access more Dock preferences (below)

Hot tip

The Apple menu is constantly available in OS X, regardless of the program in which you are working. The menu options are also constant in all applications.

Beware

You will not be able to make the Dock size too large so that some of the icons would not be visible on the desktop. By default, the Dock is resized so that everything is always visible.

...cont'd

The Dock Preferences allow you to change its size, orientation, the way icons appear and effects for when items are minimized:

The "Position on screen" options enable you to place the Dock on the left, right or bottom of the screen

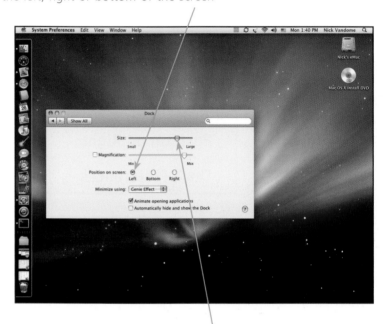

Drag the Dock Size slider to increase or decrease the size of the Dock

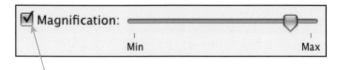

Check on the Magnification box and drag the slider to determine the size to which icons are enlarged when the cursor is moved over them

The effects that are applied to items when they are minimized is one of the features of OS X (it is not absolutely necessary but it sums up the Apple ethos of trying to enhance the user experience as much as possible).

The Genie effect shrinks the item to be minimized like a genie going back into its lamp

Hot tip

Open windows can also be minimized by double-clicking on their title bar (the thinly lined bar at the top of the window, next to the three window buttons.)

23

Manual resizing

In addition to changing the size of the Dock by using the Dock Preference dialog box, it can also be resized manually:

Drag vertically on the Dock dividing line to increase or decrease its size

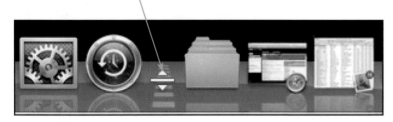

Stacks on the Dock

Stacking items

To save space on the Dock it is possible to add folders to the Dock, from where their contents can be accessed. This is known as Stacks. By default, Stacks for documents and downloaded files are created on the Dock. To use Stacks:

1 Stacked items are placed at the right-hand side of the Dock

2 Click on a Stack to view its contents

3 Stacks can be viewed as a grid, or

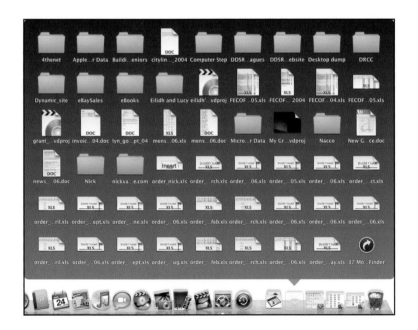

4 As a fan, depending on the number of items it contains

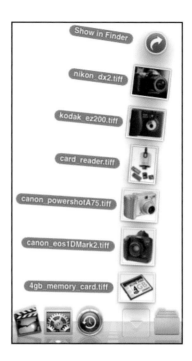

5 Click on an item within a Stack to open it

6 To create a new Stack, drag a folder onto the Dock. Any new items that are added to the folder will also be visible through the Stack

Dock menus

One of the features of the Dock is that it can display contextual menus for selected items. This means that it shows menus with options that are applicable to the item that is being accessed. This can only be done when an item has been opened.

1 Click and hold here to display an item's individual menu

✓ ☐ **OS X Leopard.doc**

Keep in Dock
Open at Login
Show in Finder
Hide
Quit

2 Click on Show in Finder to see where the item is located on your computer

Working with Dock items

Adding items

As many items as you like can be added to the Dock; the only restriction is the size of monitor in which to display all of the Dock items (the size of the Dock can be reduced to accommodate more icons but you have to be careful that all of the icons are still legible). To add items to the Dock:

Locate the required item and drag it onto the Dock. All of the other icons move along to make space for the new one

Don't forget

Icons on the Dock are shortcuts to the related item, rather than the item itself, which remains in its original location.

Keep in Dock

Every time you open a new program, its icon will appear in the Dock for the duration that the program is open, even if it has not previously been put in the Dock. If you then decide that you would like to keep it in the Dock, you can do so as follows:

Beware

You can add as many items as you like to the Dock, but it will automatically shrink to display all of its items if it becomes too big for the available space.

1 Click and hold on the icon underneath an open program

2 Click on Keep In Dock to ensure the program remains in the Dock when it is closed

...cont'd

Removing items

Any item, except the Finder, can be removed from the Dock. However, this does not remove it from our computer, it just removes the shortcut for accessing it. You will still be able to locate it in its folder on your hard drive and, if required, drag it back onto the Dock. To remove items from the Dock:

Drag it away from the Dock and release. The item disappears in a satisfying puff of smoke to indicate that it has been removed. All of the other icons then move up to fill in the space

Removing open programs

You can remove a program from the Dock, even if it is open and running. To do this:

1 Drag a program off the Dock while it is running. Initially the icon will remain on the Dock because the program is still open

2 When the program is closed its icon will be removed from the Dock (unless Keep in Dock has been selected from the item's Dock menu)

Trash

The Trash folder is a location for placing items that you do not want to use anymore. However, when items are placed in the Trash, they are not removed from your computer. This requires another command, as the Trash is really a holding area before you decide you want to remove items permanently. The Trash can also be used for ejecting removable disks attached to your Mac.

Sending items to the Trash

Items can be sent to the Trash by dragging them from the location in which they are stored:

1 Drag an item over the Trash icon to place it in the Trash folder

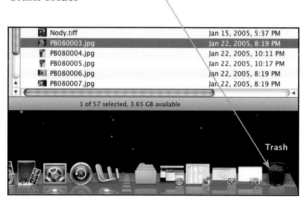

2 Click once on the Trash icon on the Dock to view its contents

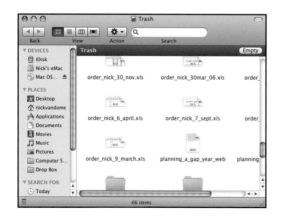

Don't forget

Items can also be sent to the Trash by selecting them and then selecting File>Move to Trash from the Menu bar.

Don't forget

All of the items within the Trash can be removed in a single command: Select Finder>Empty Trash from the Menu bar to remove all of the items in the Trash folder.

System Preferences

In OS X there are preferences that can be set for just about every aspect of the program. This gives you great control over how the interface looks and how the operating system functions. To access System Preferences:

Click on this icon on the Dock or from the Applications folder in the Finder

Personal preferences

Appearance. Options for the overall look of buttons, menus, windows and scroll bars.

Desktop & Screen Saver. This can be used to change the desktop background and the screen saver.

Dock. Options for the way the Dock looks and functions.

Exposé and Spaces. This can be used to specify keystrokes for the different Spaces and Exposé functions.

International. Options for the language used on the computer.

Security. This enables you to secure your Home folder with a master password, for added security.

Spotlight. This can be used to specify settings for the OS X search facility, Spotlight

Hardware preferences

CDs & DVDs. Options for what action is taken when you insert CDs and DVDs.

Displays. Options for the screen display, such as resolution.

Energy Saver. Options for when the computer is inactive.

Keyboard & Mouse. Options for how the keyboard and mouse function and also keyboard shortcuts.

Print & Fax. Options for selecting printers and handling faxes.

Sound. Options for adding sound effects and playing and recording sound.

Internet & Network preferences

.Mac. Options for setting up your online .Mac membership and also for configuring your iDisk. This is looked at in more detail in Chapter Seven.

Network. This can be used to specify network setting for linking two or more computers together. This is looked at in more detail in Chapter Nine.

QuickTime. Options for configuring the QuickTime Player for playing movies and music.

Sharing. This can be used to specify how files are shared over a network. This is also looked at in Chapter Nine.

System preferences

Accounts. This can be used to allow different users to create their own accounts for use on the same computer.

Date & Time. Options for changing the computer's date and time to time zones around the world.

Parental Controls. This can be used to limit access to the computer and various online functions.

Software Update. This can be used to specify how software updates are handled. It can be set so that updates are automatically downloaded when the computer is connected to the Internet, or they can be done manually.

Speech. Options for using speakable commands to control the computer. This can be useful for users who find it uncomfortable using the keyboard or the mouse as it enables them to perform some tasks by speech alone.

Startup Disk. This can be used to specify the disk from which your computer starts up. This is usually the OS X volume, or in some cases, a previous version of the Mac operating system.

Time Machine. This can be used to configure and set up the OS X backup facility.

Universal Access. This can be used to set options for users who have difficulty with viewing text on screen, hearing commands, using the keyboard or using the mouse.

Desktop items

If required, the Desktop can be used to store programs and files. However, the Finder (see Chapter Three) does such a good job of organizing all of the elements within your computer that the Desktop is rendered largely redundant, unless you feel happier storing items here. The Desktop also displays any removable disks that are connected to your computer.

Hot tip

Icons for removable disks, i.e. pen drives, CDs or DVDs, will only become visible on the Desktop once a disk has been inserted into the appropriate drive.

By default, the Desktop displays the Macintosh HD icon

If a removable disk is connected to your computer, double-click the Desktop icon to view its contents

Don't forget

Any removable disks that are connected to your computer can also be viewed by clicking on them in the Sidebar in the Finder.

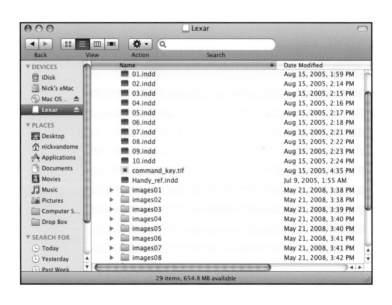

Ejecting items

If you have removable disks attached to your Mac it is essential
to be able to eject them quickly and easily. In OS X there are two
ways in which this can be done:

1   In the Finder, click on the icon
to the right of the name of the
removable disk

2   On the Desktop, drag the disk
icon over the Trash. This turns
the Trash icon into the Eject
icon and the disk will
be ejected

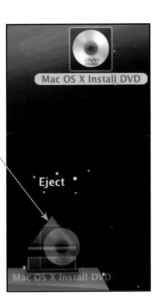

3   Some disks, such as CDs and DVDs are physically ejected
when either of these two action are performed. Other
disks, such as pen drives, have to be removed manually
once they have been ejected by OS X. If the disk is not
ejected first the following warning message will appear:

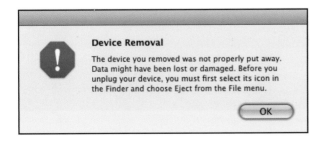

Spaces

A new way for organizing and viewing items with OS X is the Spaces feature. This enables you to specify certain areas of the screen that will contain specific content items. For instance, you can specify a space for Web content and another one for photo editing programs. To use Spaces:

1 Click on the System Preferences icon on the Dock

2 In the System Preferences folder, click on the Exposé & Spaces icon

3 Click on the Spaces tab

4 Check on the Enable Spaces box

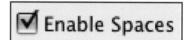

5 Check on this box to view the Spaces icon in the Finder Menu bar

6 Select the number of rows and columns you want to be displayed by Spaces

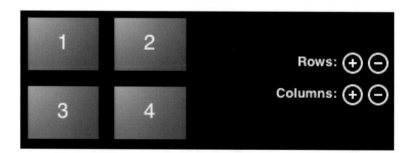

7 In the Application Assignments window, click on the Plus button

8 Select a program to be included in that assigned Space

9 Click on the Add button

10 Select the way in which you want to activate Spaces

11 Click on the assigned activation key to view the items in your Spaces

Don't forget

When you click on an area within Spaces, that content is then displayed full screen.

35

Organizing with Exposé

A similar organizational feature to Spaces is known as Exposé. This can quickly let you see what you have open on your desktop, or hide everything from view. To use Exposé:

Hot tip

Click once on any window to activate it and return it to its original size.

1 Click on the System Preferences icon on the Dock

2 In the System Preferences folder, click on the Exposé & Spaces icon

Exposé & Spaces

Hot tip

Pass the cursor over an item that has been revealed by Exposé to see its name.

3 Click on the Exposé tab

Exposé

4 Select F keys for the operation of Exposé. By default they are F9, F10 and F11

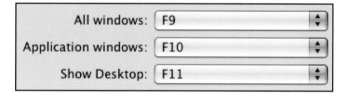

All windows:	F9
Application windows:	F10
Show Desktop:	F11

Hot tip

Press F11 to hide all of the open documents and programs on the desktop. This reveals a completely clear desktop. Press F11 again to restore all of the items.

5 Press the keys selected in Step 4 to apply that particular Exposé command

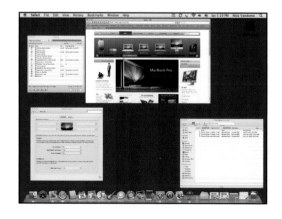

3 Finder

The principal program for moving around OS X is the Finder. This enables you to access items and organize your programs, folders and files. This chapter looks at how to use the Finder and how to get the most out of this powerful tool that is at the heart of navigating around OS X. It covers accessing items through the Finder, how to customize the interface and numerous options for working with folders in OS X.

Working with the Finder

If you were only able to use one item on the Dock it would be the Finder. This is the gateway to all of the elements of your computer. It is possible to get to selected items through other routes, but the Finder is the only location where you can gain access to everything on your system. If you ever feel that you are getting lost within OS X, click on the Finder and then you should begin to feel more at home. To access the Finder:

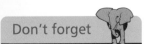

Don't forget

The Finder is always open (as denoted by the graphic underneath its icon on the Dock) and it cannot readily be closed down or removed.

Click once on this icon on the Dock

Overview

The Finder has its own toolbar, a Sidebar from which items can be accessed and a main window where the contents of selected items can be viewed:

Don't forget

The Action button has options for displaying information about a selected item and also options for how it is displayed with the Finder.

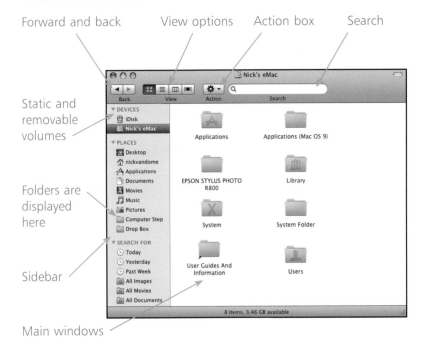

Forward and back   View options   Action box   Search

Static and removable volumes

Folders are displayed here

Sidebar

Main windows

Finder folders

Home

This contains the contents of your own home directory, containing your personal folders and files. OS X inserts some pre-named folders which it thinks will be useful, but it is possible to rename, rearrange or delete these as you please. It is also possible to add as many more folders as you want.

1 Click on this link in the Finder Sidebar to access the contents of your Home folder

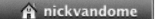

2 The Home folder contains the Public folder that can be used to share files with other users if the computer is part of a network

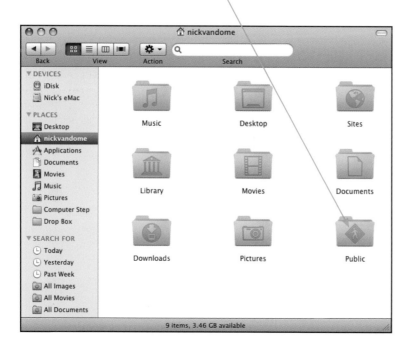

Hot tip

Your Home folder is a good one to add to the Dock, so that all of your own programs, folders and files are accessible with a single click.

Hot tip

When you are creating documents OS X, by default, recognizes their type and then, when you save them, suggests the most applicable folder in your Home directory in which to save them. So, if you have created a word processed document, OS X will suggest you save it in Documents, if it is a photograph it will suggest Pictures, if it is a video it will suggest Movies, and so on.

...cont'd

Applications

This folder contains some of the programs on your computer. However, by default, it is only the programs that come installed with OS X and not every program on your system. If you had programs that you used under a previous Mac operating system, these will be contained within the Applications (Mac OS 9) folder which can be accessed directly from your hard drive in the Finder. However, it is possible to add any of these programs to your Applications folder by opening the Applications (Mac OS 9) folder and then dragging items into the Applications folder.

40

1 Click on this link in the Finder Sidebar to access the contents of your Applications folder

2 Double-click on an application icon to open the relevant program. This will open in its own, new, window

Finder views

The way in which items are displayed within the Finder can be amended in a variety of ways, depending on how you want to view the contents of a folder. Different folders can have their own viewing options applied to them and these will stay in place until a new option is specified.

Back button

When working within the Finder each new window replaces the previous one, unless you open a new program. This prevents the screen becoming cluttered with dozens of open windows, as you look through various Finder windows for a particular item. To ensure that you never feel lost within the Finder structure, there is a Back button on the Finder toolbar that enables you to retrace the steps that you have taken.

Beware

If you have not opened any Finder windows, the Back button will not operate at all.

1 Navigate to a folder within the Finder (in this case the "For printing" folder contained within Pictures)

2 Click on the Back button to move back to the previously visited window (in this case, the main Pictures window)

Icon view

One of the viewing options for displaying items within the Finder is as icons. This provides a graphical representation of the items in the Finder. It is possible to customize the way that Icon view looks and functions:

Hot tip

The Arrange By options can be used to arrange icons into specific groups, e.g. by name or type, or to snap them to an invisible grid so that they have an ordered appearance.

1 Click here on the Finder toolbar to access Icon view

2 Select View from the Menu bar, check on "as Icons" and select "Show View Options" to access the options for customizing Icon view

42

Hot tip

A very large icon size can be useful for people with poor eyesight, but it does take up a lot more space in a window.

Drag this slider to set the icon size

Select an option for the way icons are arranged in Finder windows

Select an option for the background of the Finder window

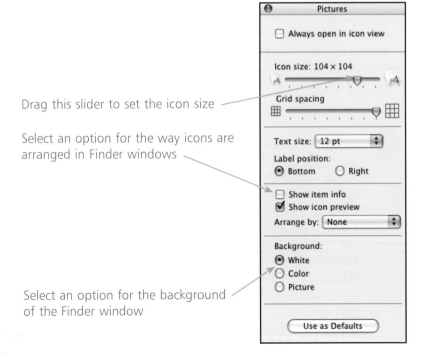

List view

List view can be used to show the items within a Finder window as a list, with additional information shown next to them. This can be a more efficient method than icon view if there are a lot of items within a folder: List view enables you to see more items at one time and also view the additional information.

1 Click here on the Finder toolbar to access List view

2 The name of each folder or file is displayed here. If any item has additional elements within it, this is represented by a small triangle next to them. Additional information in List view, such as file size and last modified date, is included in columns to the right

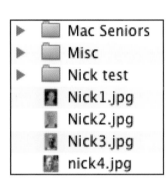

Column view

Column view is a useful option if you want to trace the location of a particular item, i.e. see the full path of its location, starting from the hard drive.

1 Click here on the Finder toolbar to access Column view

2 Click on an item to see everything within that folder. If an arrow follows an item it means that there are further items to view

Covers

Covers is another innovative feature on the Mac, that enables you to view the contents of a folder without having to open the folder itself. Additionally, each item is displayed as a large icon that enables you to see what a particular item contains, such as images. To use Covers:

1 Select a folder and at the top of the Finder window click on this button

2 The items within the folder are displayed in their cover state

3 Drag with the mouse on each item to view the next one, or click on the slider at the bottom of the window

Quick Look

Through a Finder option called Quick Look, it is possible to view the content of a file without having to first open it. To do this:

1 Select a file within the Finder

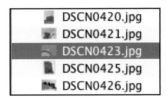

2 Press the space bar

3 The contents of the file are displayed without it opening in its default program

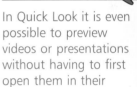

Hot tip

In Quick Look it is even possible to preview videos or presentations without having to first open them in their default program.

4 Click on the cross to close Quick Look

45

Finder toolbar

Customizing the toolbar

As with most elements of OS X, it is possible to customize the Finder toolbar:

1   Select View>Customize Toolbar from the Menu bar

2   Drag items from the window into the toolbar, or:

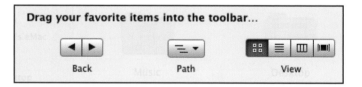

3   Drag the default set of icons into the toolbar

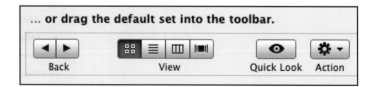

4   Click Done at the bottom of the window

Finder Sidebar

Using the Sidebar

The Sidebar is the left-hand panel of the Finder which can be used to access items on your Mac:

1 Click on an item on the Sidebar

2 Its contents are displayed in the main Finder window

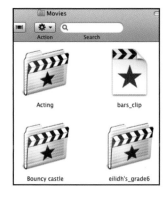

Adding to the Sidebar

Items that you access most frequently can be added to the Sidebar. To do this:

1 Drag an item from the main Finder window onto the Sidebar

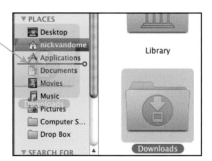

2 The item is added to the Sidebar. You can do this with programs, folders and files

Don't forget

When you click on an item in the Sidebar, its contents are shown in the main Finder window to its right.

Don't forget

When items are added to the Finder Sidebar a shortcut, or alias, is inserted into the Sidebar, not the actual item.

Don't forget

Items can be removed from the Sidebar by dragging them away from it. They then disappear in a satisfying puff of smoke. This does not remove the item from your Mac, just the Finder Sidebar.

Finder search

Searching electronic data is now a massive industry, with companies such as Google leading the way with online searching. On Macs it is also possible to search your folders and files, using the built-in search facilities. This can be done either through the Finder or with the Spotlight program (see Chapter Five).

Using Finder
To search for items within the Finder:

Don't forget

Try and make your search keywords and phrases as accurate as possible. This will create a better list of search results.

1 In the Finder window, enter the search keyword(s) in this box

2 The results are shown in the Finder window

3 Select the areas over which you want the search performed

Don't forget

Both folders and files will be displayed in the Finder as part of the search results.

4 Double-click on a folder to see its contents

5 Double-click on a file to open it

6 Click once on an item to view its file path on your computer (i.e. where it is actually located)

Creating aliases

Aliases are shortcuts to the actual version of items. This can include programs, folders and files. Aliases take up virtually no disk space and numerous aliases can be created for a single item and then placed in various locations for ease of access. To create an alias:

1 Select an item in any open window, by clicking on it once

2 Select File>Make Alias from the Menu bar

3 Once an alias has been created, it can then be moved to any location (in this case the Desktop)

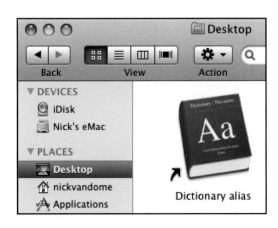

Dictionary alias

Copying and moving items

Items can be copied and moved within OS X by using the copy and paste method or by dragging:

Copy and paste

1 Select an item and select Edit> Copy from the Menu bar

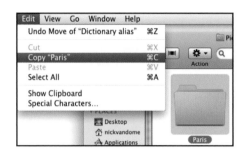

2 Move to the target location and select Edit>Paste Item from the Menu bar. The item is then pasted into the new location

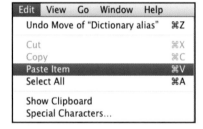

Dragging

Drag a file from one location into another to move it to that location

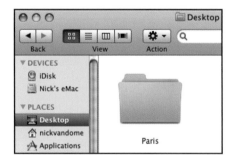

Working with windows

OS X has a much better method of managing open windows than any of the previous Apple operating systems. Whenever a new item is accessed from within the Finder, it replaces the existing window, rather than opening a new window. This means that the screen does not become cluttered with a lot of open windows. The exception to this is programs, which always open in their own, new window.

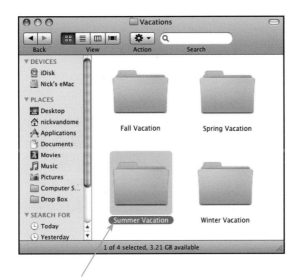

Don't forget

Use the Back button to move back to the most recently accessed window.

51

From within the Finder, if you select a new item (except a program) it replaces the existing item, rather than opening in a new window

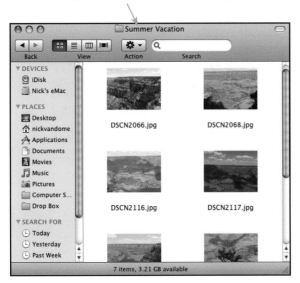

...cont'd

When you are working with a lot of open windows it can sometimes be confusing about which is the active window and how you can then quickly switch to other windows.

1 The active window always sits on the top of any other open windows. There can only be one active window at any one time

If you hold down the Command key, (the one with the Apple symbol on it), you can drag a background window without bringing it to the front.

2 Click on any window behind the currently active one, to bring it to the front and make it active

3 At the top left of any active window, click on the red button to close it, the amber button to minimize it and the green button to enlarge it

Working with folders

When OS X is first installed, there are various folders that have already been created to hold programs and files. Some of these are essential (i.e. those containing programs) while others are created as an aid for where you might want to store the files that you create (such as the Pictures and Movies folders). Once you start working with OS X you will probably want to create your own folders, in which to store and organize your documents. This can be done on the desktop or within any level of your existing folder structure. To create a new folder:

1 Access the location in which you want to create the new folder (i.e. your Home folder) and select File>New Folder from the Menu bar

2 A new, empty, folder is inserted at the selected location (named "untitled folder")

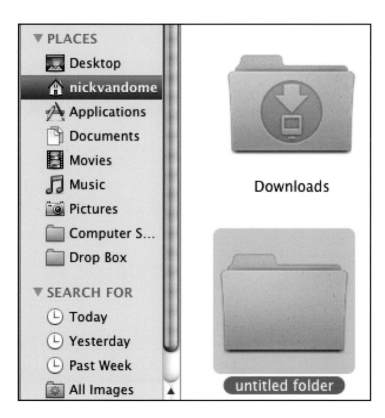

Don't forget

Folders are always denoted by a folder icon. This is the same regardless of the Finder view which is selected. The only difference is that the icon is larger in Icon view than in List or Column views.

53

...cont'd

3 Overtype the file name with a new one. Press Enter

4 Double-click on a folder to view its contents (at this point it should be empty)

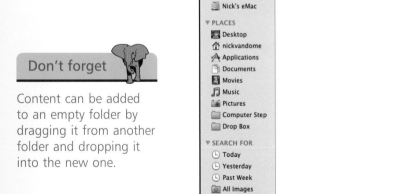

Smart Folders

When working on any computer it is inevitable that you will soon have a number of related files in different locations. This could be because you save your images in one folder, your word processing documents in another, web pages in another and so on. This can cause difficulties when you are trying to keep track of a lot of related documents. OS X overcomes this problem through the use of Smart Folders. These are folders that you set up using Finder search results as the foundation. Then when new items are created that meet the original criteria they are automatically included within the Smart Folder. To create a Smart Folder:

Hot tip

Numerous different Smart Folders can be created, for different types of files and information.

1 Conduct a search with the Finder search box

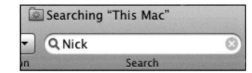

2 Once the search is completed, click the Save button to create a Smart Folder

Save

3 Enter a name for the new Smart Folder and click Save

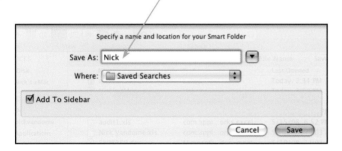

4 The Smart Folder is added to the Finder Sidebar. Click the Smart Folder to view its contents

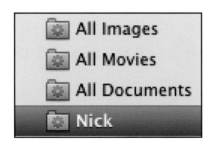

...cont'd

5 Create a new item that matches some, or all, of the original search criteria

Nick's stuff

6 The new item is automatically included within the Smart Folder

56

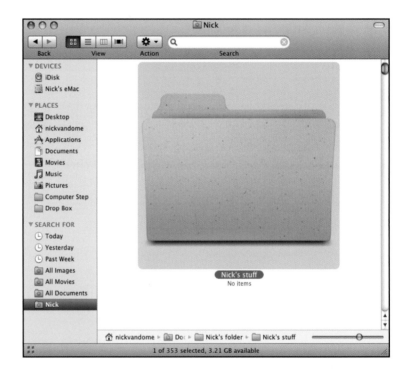

7 Click on an item to view its full path

nickvandome ▸ Doc ▸ Nick's folder ▸ Nick's stuff

Spring-loaded folders

Another method for moving items with the Finder is to use the spring-loaded folder option. This enables you to drag items into a folder and then view the contents of the folder before you drop the item into it. This means that you can drag items into nested folders in a single operation. To do this:

1 Select the item you want to move

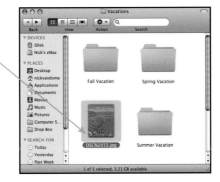

2 Drag the selected item over the folder into which you want to place it. Keep the mouse held down

3 The folder will open, revealing its contents. The selected item can either be dropped into the folder or, if there are sub-folders, the same operation can be repeated until you find the folder into which you want to place the selected item

Hot tip

The spring-loaded folder technique can be used to move items between different locations within the Finder, e.g. for moving files from your Pictures folder into your Home folder.

Beware

Do not release the mouse button until you have reached the location into which you want to place the selected item.

Burnable folders

With the increasing use of images, digital video and music files, computer users are frequently copying data from their computers onto CDs. In some cases this can be a frustrating process but in OS X the use of burnable folders can make the process much quicker. These are folders that can be created specifically for the contents to be burned onto a CD or DVD. To do this:

1 In the Finder, select File>New Burn Folder from the Menu bar

2 The burn folder is created in the Finder window which was active when Step 1 was performed. Click on the folder name and overtype to give it a unique name

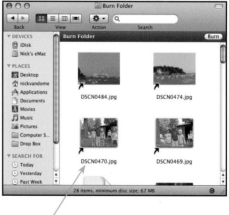

3 Select the items that you want to burn and drag and drop or copy and paste them into the burn folder

4 Click here to burn the disk

Selecting items

Programs and files within OS X folders can be selected by a variety of different methods:

Selecting by dragging
Drag the cursor to encompass the items to be selected. The selected items will become highlighted.

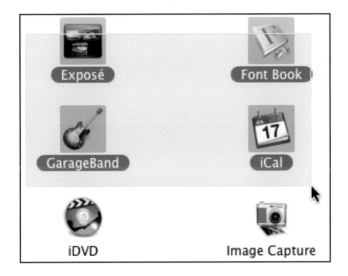

Selecting by clicking
Click once on an item to select it, hold down Shift and then click on another item in a list to select a consecutive group of items.

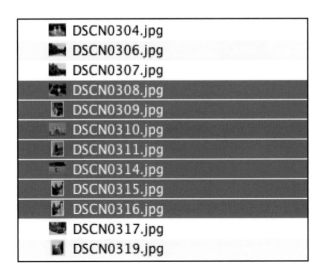

...cont'd

To select a non-consecutive group, select the first item by clicking on it once, then hold down the Command key (the one with the Apple symbol on it) and select the other required items. The selected items will appear highlighted.

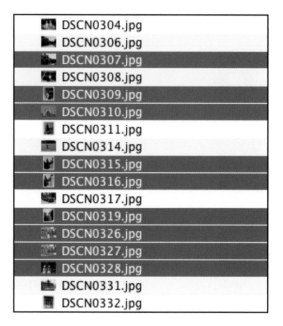

> **Don't forget**
>
> The Select All command selects all of the elements within the active item. For instance, if the active item is a word processing document, the Select All command will select all of the items within the document; if it is a folder it will select all of the items within that folder.

Select All

To select all of the items in a folder, select Edit>Select All from the Menu bar:

Labeling items

With the Finder it is possible to label items (including files, folders and programs) so that they can easily be identified for specific purposes. This could be for items that were created on a certain date or to quickly identify a particular type of document. To do this:

1 Select an item, or group of items, to which you want to apply labels

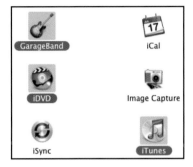

Don't forget

Labels are visible regardless of the View option that is selected in the Finder.

2 Click the Actions button and select a color for the label, or labels

3 The colored labels are applied to the selected items. Other items can then have other label colors applied to them

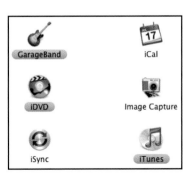

Menus

The main Apple menu bar in OS X contains a variety of menus, which are consistent regardless of the program in operation:

- Apple menu. This is denoted by a translucent blue apple and contains general information about the computer, a preferences option for changing the functionality and appearance of the Dock and options for closing down the computer

- Finder menu. This contains preferences options for amending the functionality and appearance of the Finder and also options for emptying the Trash and accessing other programs (under the Services option)

- File menu. This contains common commands for working with open documents, such as opening and closing files, creating aliases, moving to the Trash, ejecting external devices and burning discs

- Edit menu. This contains common commands that apply to the majority of programs used on the Mac. These include undo, cut, copy, paste, select all and show the contents of the clipboard, i.e. items that have been cut or copied

- View. This contains options for how windows and folders are displayed within the Finder and for customizing the Finder toolbar

- Go. This can be used to navigate around your computer. This includes moving to your Home folder, your iDisk, your Applications folder, recently opened items and also remote servers for connecting to other computers on a network

- Window. This contains commands to organize the currently open programs and files on your desktop

- Help. This contains the Mac Help files which contain information about all aspects of OS X

4 Digital lifestyle

Leisure time, and how we use it, is a significant issue for everyone. Within the OS X environment there are several programs that can be used to create and manage your digital lifestyle. Some of these are known as the iLife suite of programs and cover photos, music, home movies, DVD creation, creating websites and composing music.

iPhoto

iPhoto is the photo management program for OS X. The intention of iPhoto is to make the organizing, manipulation and sharing of digital images as easy as possible. To begin using iPhoto and downloading photos:

1 Click once on this icon on the Dock

2 Connect your digital camera, or card reader, to your Mac via either USB or Firewire. The images on the connected device are displayed in the main iPhoto window

3 Click on the Import All button to import all of the images from the camera, or card reader

Import All...

4 Select specific images and click on the Import Selected button

Import Selected

Once photographs have been downloaded by iPhoto they are displayed within the Library. This is the main storage area for all of the photographs that are added to iPhoto.

Viewing photos

There are a variety of ways in which photos can be viewed and displayed in iPhoto:

1 In the main window double-click on an image

2 This displays it at full size (click on it once to return to the main window)

Hot tip

Zooming right in on a photo is an excellent way to view fine detail and see if the photo is properly in focus.

3 In the main window drag this slider to display images in the main iPhoto window at different sizes

Creating a photo album

One of the first things to do in iPhoto is to create different albums (or folders) for your photographs. This is because the number of photographs will expand quickly and it is important to have different locations for different subject matter. This will make it a lot easier to organize your photographs and find the ones you want quickly. To create a new album:

1 Under the Source panel, click on the Add button

2 Enter a name for the new album

3 Click on the Create button

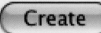

4 The new album is added in the Source panel

5 To add photos to an album, click on the Photos button under the Library heading

6 Select the photos you want to use in the album

Don't forget

Once photos have been added to an album they are still visible in the main Library. The items in each album are just a reference back to the Library items.

7 Drag the photos into the album

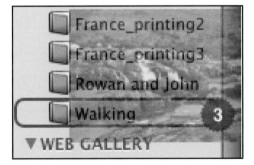

France_printing2
France_printing3
Rowan and John
Walking   3
▼ WEB GALLERY

Beware

If you delete a photo from the Library it will also be deleted from any albums in which it has been placed. But if a photo is deleted from an album it is still available in the Library.

8 Click on an album to view its contents in the main iPhoto window

67

Enhancing your photos

One of the great advantages of digital photos is that they can be edited and enhanced in numerous ways. Although iPhoto is primarily an organizational tool for digital photos, it also serves as a photo editor.

Some basic editing functions can be applied in iPhoto and in each case the process is similar:

1 Click on the Edit button

2 Apply an editing function and click on the Apply button

The editing functions that can be applied are:

1 Click on this button to crop a photo by dragging over the area you want to keep

Don't forget

Most photos will benefit from some degree of cropping.

2 Click on this button to adjust color properties such as exposure and brightness and contrast

Beware

Be careful not to overdo color adjustments as this can give a photo an unnatural look.

3 Click on this button to remove red-eye by clicking on the affected area

4 Click on this button to add effects such as sepia tone

Sharing your photos

iPhoto offers a number of creative ways in which you can share your photos:

1 Click on this button to share selected photos on an online Web Gallery

Hot tip

For more information about Web Galleries see Chapter Seven.

2 Click on this button to share selected photos creatively in an email

3 Click on this button to print selected photos

4 Click on this button to set a selected photo as your current desktop background image

Don't forget

The Order Prints button will automatically connect you to an online printing service appropriate to your current location.

5 Click on this button to order prints from an online service

iTunes

Music is one of the areas that has revived Apple's fortunes in recent years, primarily through the iPod music player and iTunes; and also the iTunes music store, where music can be bought online. iTunes is a versatile program but its basic function is to play a music CD. To do this:

1 Insert the CD in the CD/DVD drive

2 By default, iTunes will open and display this window. Click No if you just want to play the CD

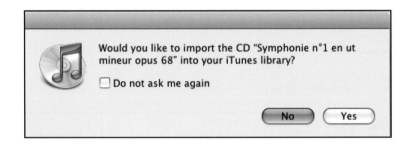

Would you like to import the CD "Symphonie n°1 en ut mineur opus 68" into your iTunes library?

☐ Do not ask me again

No   Yes

3 Click on the CD name

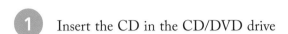

▼ DEVICES
Symphonie n°1 ...

4 Click on this button to play the whole CD

5 Click on the Import CD button if you want to copy the music from the CD onto your hard drive

Import CD

70

Organizing your music

iTunes offers great flexibility when it comes to organizing your music.

1 Click here to view all of the music in your iTunes Library

2 Click on this button to display a quick view of your iTunes music

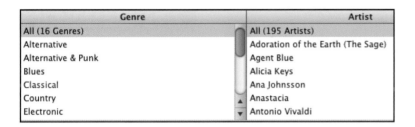

Genre	Artist
All (16 Genres)	All (195 Artists)
Alternative	Adoration of the Earth (The Sage)
Alternative & Punk	Agent Blue
Blues	Alicia Keys
Classical	Ana Johnsson
Country	Anastacia
Electronic	Antonio Vivaldi

3 Click on this button to view your iTunes Library according to the relevant covers for the music

Shaka Zulu
Ladysmith Black Mambazo

Don't forget

Move through the covers in the library by dragging horizontally on each cover, or use the slider below the covers.

4 Click on this button to play all of the music in your iTunes Library in a random order

...cont'd

Adding a playlist

A playlist in iTunes is a selection of music that you want to group together under certain headings, such as for a party or a certain mood or genre. To create a playlist:

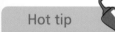 Click on this button at the bottom of the Library section panel

Hot tip

Once you have created a playlist you can then burn this onto a CD.

2 Enter a name for the new playlist

3 Click on the required items of music in the main window

4 Drag the selected items over the playlist folder and release

5 The selected items are included in the playlist

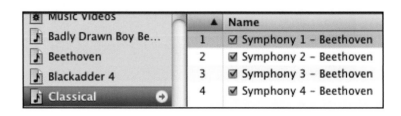

Downloading music

As well as playing music, iTunes can also be used to legally download music, via the iTunes Store. This contains a huge range of music and you have to register on the site once. After this you can download music for use on your Mac and also for downloading onto an iPod. To do this:

1 Under the Library section in iTunes, click on the iTunes Store button

2 The iTunes Store offers music, videos, television programs, audiobooks and podcasts for downloading

Beware

Never use illegal music download sites. Apart from the legal factor, they are much more likely to contain viruses and spyware.

3 Look for items in the iTunes Store either by browsing through the sections of the site, or enter a keyword in the search box at the top of the window

...cont'd

4 Locate an item you want to buy

5 Click on the Buy button (at this point you will have to register with the iTunes Store, if you have not already done so)

6 Once you have registered, you will have to enter a username and password to complete your purchase

7 Once the item has been downloaded it is available through iTunes on your Mac, under the Purchased button

Adding an iPod

Since their introduction in 2001 iPods have become an inescapable part of modern life. It is impossible to sit on a bus or a train without seeing someone with the ubiquitous white earbuds, humming away to their favorite tunes. iPods are for everyone and they are designed to work seamlessly with iTunes and the latter can be used to load music onto the former. To do this:

1 Connect your iPod to the Mac with the supplied USB or Firewire cable

2 iTunes will open automatically and display details about the attached iPod

Don't forget

iPods come in a variety of styles, colors, sizes and disc capacity.

75

3 iTunes should automatically start copying music from the iTunes Library onto the iPod. If not, select the iPod under the Devices heading

4 Select File>Sync from the iTunes Menu bar to synchronize iTunes and your iPod

iMovie

For home movie buffs, iMovie offers options for downloading, editing and publishing your efforts:

1 Click on this button on the Dock

2 Attach a digital video camera to your Mac with a Firewire cable

3 Click here to access the camera

4 Click here to play the video in the camera

5 Click on the Import button to copy the video into iMovie

6 Click on the Done button to return to the editing environment

7 Downloaded video clips are shown here

8 Drag a clip into the project window to add it to a new video project

9 Click on this button to access Transition options

Don't forget

Transitions are graphical elements that are placed between two movie clips.

10 Click on this button to access Text options

Don't forget

Video clips can be edited by selecting them in the project window and then clicking on the Trim Clip button at the bottom left of the clip. The clip can then be trimmed by dragging the beginning or the end of the clip.

11 Click on this button to access Sound options

12 Text, transitions and sound can be added to a movie by dragging them between the video clips

13 Click Share on the Menu bar and select an option for exporting the finished movie

iDVD

Once video has been created, it can be shared amongst family and friends on a DVD. This can be done through the iDVD program. To do this:

1 Click on this icon on the Dock

2 Click on the Create a New Project option

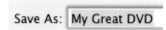

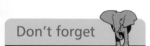

Don't forget

All of your photos in iPhoto and music in iTunes are available to include in the DVD, through the audio and photos tabs.

3 Give the project a name

4 Click on the Create button

5 Click on the Themes button

6 Double-click on a theme to select it as the background of your DVD

7 Click on the Media button

Media

8 Click on the Photos tab

Photos

9 Select a photo and drag it onto the Drop Zones of the theme

Don't forget

If Drop Zones are left empty a warning will appear when you try and burn the final DVD. However, this can safely be ignored.

10 Click on the Movie tab

Movies

11 Select a movie and drag it onto the Theme

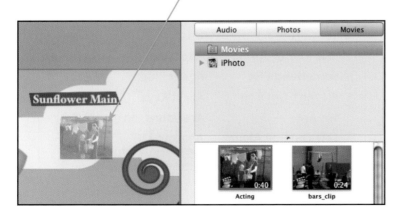

...cont'd

12 Click on the movie
name and type a new
name if required

13 Click on the Audio tab

Audio

14 Select an audio element that you want to use as
background music for the DVD and drag it
onto the Theme

15 Click on this button to edit the Drop Zone

Don't forget

Drop zones can be edited by adding different photos.

16 Click on this button to view the animation of the Theme

17 Click on this button to preview the project

Hot tip

Burn DVDs at a slower speed than the maximum available. This will ensure a better chance of it being burned correctly.

18 Click on this button to burn the completed DVD

iWeb

It seems as if everybody has their own websites these days. Not only are they a great way to publish family information, they are also ideal for clubs or charity organizations. With the online .Mac service and a program called iWeb it is possible to quickly get up and running on the Web with your own site. To do this:

Don't forget

For more information about the .Mac service, see Chapter Seven.

1 Click on the iWeb icon on the Dock, or select it in the Applications folder

2 Select a template for the design of your website

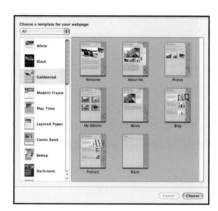

Hot tip

For a website, a clear, simple design is usually the most effective, particularly over a period of time.

3 Click on the Choose button

4 Click on a text item and overtype to change it

82

5 Click on the Media button at the bottom of the window

6 Click on the Photos tab and select a photo

7 Drag the photo onto one of the existing photo placeholders

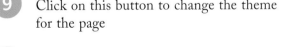

Beware

8 Your own photo replaces the current item

Photos can be resized on an iWeb page, but do not make them too big or else they may take up too much space.

9 Click on this button to change the theme for the page

10 Click on this button to add a text box (by dragging) on the page

11 Click on this button to add shapes to the page

...cont'd

12 To add a new page, select File>New Page from the iWeb Menu bar, or click on the Add button under the Site panel

13 In the Site panel, click on the names of each page to move between them

14 Click on the Publish button to publish the site to your .Mac account

15 The following message will appear. Click on Continue

16 Once your website has been published the following message appears

17 Click on the Announce button to invite family and friends to view your site

18 An email is generated with this message pre-inserted. Add email recipients and send the message to them. When they receive it they will be able to follow a link to your website

GarageBand

For those who are as interested in creating music as listening to it, GarageBand can be used for this very purpose. It can take a bit of time and practice to become fully proficient with GarageBand but it is worth persevering with if you are musically inclined and want to compose your own. To use GarageBand:

1 Click on this icon on the Dock or double-click on it in the Applications folder

2 Select File>New from the GarageBand Menu Bar

3 Click on the Create New Music Project button

Don't forget

GarageBand can appear quite complex at first and it takes a little bit of time to feel comfortable with it.

85

4 Give your new song a name and select any relevant settings. Click on the Create button

5 Click on this button to view available loops of music

6 Click on an instrument type to see the available options

...cont'd

7 Drag a loop here to add it to a song

8 Select a loop and click on the keyboard to create your own music with that instrument

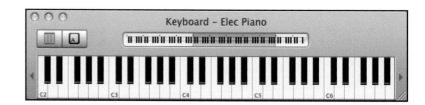

9 Use the mixer to mix each individual track

10 Select File>Save from the Menu bar to save your composition

5 Getting productive

In addition to the digital lifestyle types of programs, there are several other applications within OS X that can be used to create, store and display information. This chapter shows how to access and use these programs, so that you can get the most out of OS X as an efficient and productive work tool.

Dashboard

The OS X Dashboard is a collection of widgets within OS X that can be used for common tasks such as a calendar, an address book and a dictionary. To use the Dashboard:

1 Click once on this icon on the Dock

2 The Dashboard widgets are maximized on the screen and superimposed over the rest of the active programs

Hot tip

By default, the Dashboard widgets can be accessed quickly by pressing F12.

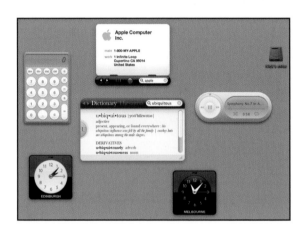

Beware

Some widgets, such as the one for weather around the world, require an active Internet connection.

3 Click here to view the panel of all of the available widgets (by default, only a selection are visible when the Dashboard is accessed)

4 The full range of widgets are shown here

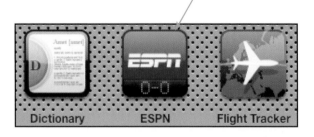

5 To make a widget active, drag it from the Dashboard panel onto the main window

Adding Dashboard widgets

In order to maximize the benefit of the Dashboard, Apple have encourage developers to create and publish their own widgets. This has resulted in dozens of new widgets that can be downloaded from the Apple website at www.apple.com/downloads/dashboard/. From here, the available widgets can be viewed and downloaded:

1 Click here to download specific widgets

2 Click here to view the top downloads

3 Scroll down the downloads page and click here to view available widgets by category

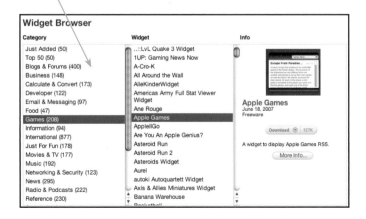

Spotlight search

Spotlight is the Mac's dedicated search program. It can be used over the files on your Mac. To use Spotlight:

1 Click on this icon at the far right of the Finder Menu bar

2 In the Spotlight box, enter the search keyword(s)

Don't forget

Since the Spotlight search is always visible, it can be a quicker way to look for items than the Finder search.

3 The results are displayed according to type

Beware

Spotlight starts searching for items as soon as you start typing a word. So don't worry if some of the first results look inappropriate as these will disappear once you have finished typing the full word.

4 Click on an item to view it or see its contents (in the case of folders)

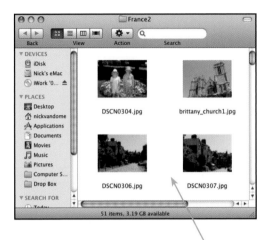

5 If you select a folder, it will be displayed in its location within the Finder

6 Click on the Spotlight Preferences link

Spotlight Preferences...

7 Order the different content types according to how you would like them displayed in the Spotlight search results

Address Book

The Address Book can be used to store contact information, which can then be used in different applications and even published on the Web so that you can access it from computers around the world.

Overview

The Address Book contains contact information, either for groups or for individuals. The Address Book can display this information in two ways:

1 Click here to view card and column information

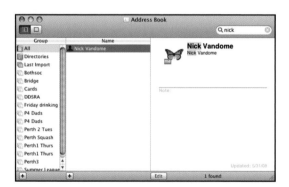

2 Click here to view card information only i.e. individual Address Book entries

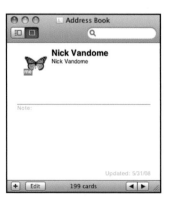

Adding contact information

The main function of the Address Book is to include details of personal and business contacts. This has to be done manually for each entry, but it can prove to be a valuable resource once it has been completed. To add contact information:

1 Click here to edit contact information

2 Click on a category and enter contact information. Press Tab to move to the next field. Click the green button to access additional options for a certain category

> **Don't forget**
>
> Different types of entries have different icons next to them. The entry for the computer's administrator is a black silhouette rather than an index card used for a standard entry.

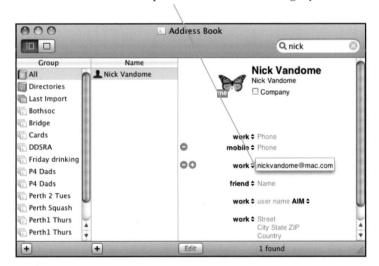

3 Click here and browse your hard drive to add a photograph for the selected contact

...cont'd

Adding personal contacts

Click on the Plus button. Create a new contact and enter the information here. Make sure the Company box is checked off

Adding business contacts

Create a new contact and check on the Company box. Business contacts and personal contacts have different icons

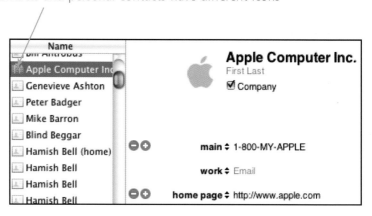

Creating groups

In addition to creating individual entries in the Address Book, group contacts can also be created. This is a way of grouping contacts with similar interests. Once a group has been created, all of the entries within it can be accessed and contacted by selecting the relevant entry under the Group column. To create a group:

1 Click on this button under the Group panel to create a new group entry

2 Give the new group a name

3 Drag individual entries into the group (the individual entries are retained too)

4 Click on a group name to view the members of the group

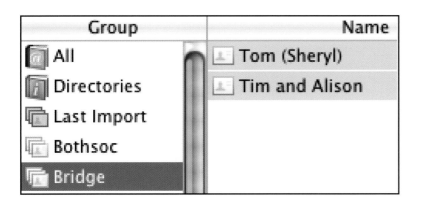

Hot tip

Individual and group entries in Address Book can be used within the OS X email program, Mail. When you enter names in the email To box the relevant options from the Address Book will be displayed.

Beware

Individuals can be included in several groups. However, if you change their details in one group these changes will take effect across all of the groups in which the entry occurs.

95

iCal

Electronic calendars are now a standard part of modern life and with OS X this function is performed by the iCal program. Not only can this be used on your Mac, it can also be synchronized with other Apple devices such as an iPod or an iPhone. To create a calendar:

1 Click on this icon on the Dock, or double-click on it in the Applications folder in the Finder

2 Click on the Today button to view the current day

Today

3 Select whether to view the calendar by day, week or month

4 Select a date and Ctrl+click

5 Select New Event

6 Enter the details for the new event

7 Double-click on an item and select options for how it is displayed

Creating more calendars

It is also possible to create color-coded calendars for different events or activities. To do this:

1 Under the Calendars section, click on this button

2 The new calendar is highlighted as Untitled

Hot tip

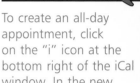

To create an all-day appointment, click on the "i" icon at the bottom right of the iCal window. In the new panel, check on the "all-day" box.

3 Enter a name for the new calendar

4 When you make a new entry, select the appropriate calendar first. Then the entry will take on the calendar's designated color

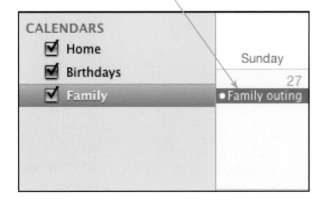

...cont'd

Mini Calendars

There are also options for displaying a mini calendar

 Click here to show the mini calendar

Click on the arrows at the top to move through the months

◄		August 2008				►
Sun	Mon	Tue	Wed	Thu	Fri	Sat
27	28	29	30	31	1	2
3	4	5	6	7	8	9
10	11	12	13	14	15	16
17	18	19	20	21	22	23
24	25	26	27	28	29	30
31	1	2	3	4	5	6

Drag here to expand the mini calendar view

◄		August 2008				►
Sun	Mon	Tue	Wed	Thu	Fri	Sat
27	28	29	30	31	1	2
3	4	5	6	7	8	9
10	11	12	13	14	15	16
17	18	19	20	21	22	23
24	25	26	27	28	29	30
31						

		September 2008				
Sun	Mon	Tue	Wed	Thu	Fri	Sat
	1	2	3	4	5	6
7	8	9	10	11	12	13
14	15	16	17	18	19	20
21	22	23	24	25	26	27
28	29	30				

To Do list

iCal also contains a To Do list, to which you can add reminders for tasks that have to be completed. To do this:

1 Click here to show the To Do list

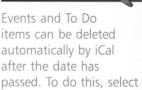

2 Under the To Do items heading, Ctrl+click and select New To Do

3 Enter the required To Do item

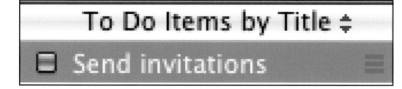

Font Book

The Font Book is an application that can be used to add, organize and remove fonts within OS X. To use the Font Book:

Viewing fonts

The available fonts on the system can be viewed via the Font Book:

Click on a Collection and a Font. An example is displayed here

Don't forget

To open the Font Book, click on this icon on the Dock or in the Applications folder:

Adding fonts

New fonts can be added through Font Book and existing fonts can be disabled throughout your computer. To do this:

1 Click here to add a new font

2 Click here to disable an existing font

Preview

Preview is an OS X application that can be used to view multiple file types, particularly image file formats. This can be useful if you just want to view documents without editing them in a dedicated program, such as an image editing program. Preview can also be used to view PDF (Portable Document Format) files and also preview documents before they are printed. To use Preview:

1 Double-click on an item within the Finder

2 The selected file is displayed by Preview

Don't forget

To open the Preview, click on this icon on the Dock or in the Applications folder:

Hot tip

If you want to edit digital images use either iPhoto or an image editing program such as Photoshop Elements from Adobe.

iWork

iWork is a suite of productivity programs designed specifically for OS X. It is similar to the Microsoft Office suite and contains a word processor program, a spreadsheet program, and a presentation program. To use iWork:

1 Once iWork has been installed, double-click on the iWork folder in the Applications folder

2 Click on this icon to access the word processing function

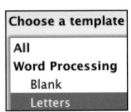

Don't forget

iWork does not come with Mac computers running OS X and has to be bought separately.

3 Select an option for the type of document you want to create

4 There are numerous templates that can be used for items such as letters

5 There are also templates for more complex items such as newsletters

Family Newsletter

6 Click on this icon to access the spreadsheet function

Numbers

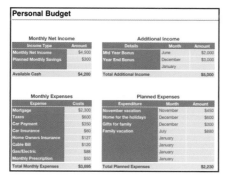

103

7 Click on this icon to access the presentation function

Keynote

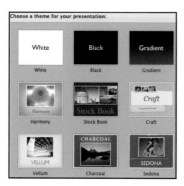

OS X applications

Most of the frequently used OS X programs are located in the Applications folder:

Don't forget

Image Capture can be used to download images from a digital device, unless you have set iPhoto to be the default for performing this task.

Some of the applications (excluding those in this chapter) include:

- Automator. This can be used to automate repetitive tasks

- Chess. Play online chess against your Mac computer

- Dictionary. A digital dictionary

- Front Row. A program for accessing music, movies or photos with a remote control

- Image Capture. A program for transferring images from a digital camera or scanner

- QuickTime Player. The default application for viewing video

- iPhoto, iTunes, iMovie, iDVD, iWeb and GarageBand. The digital lifestyle programs for working with photos, music, home movies and websites

- Safari. The OS X specific Web browser

- Mail. The default email program

- Stickies. A small program for adding note-like reminders

- TextEdit. A program for editing text files

- Time Machine. OS X's backup facility

OS X utilities

In addition to the programs in the Applications folder, there are also a number of utility programs that perform a variety of tasks within OS X. To access the Utilities:

1 Open the Applications folder and double-click on the Utilities folder

2 The available utilities are displayed within the Utilities folder

...cont'd

- Activity Monitor. This contains information about the system memory being used and disk activity (see Chapter Ten for more details)

- AirPort Admin Utility. This can be used if you have an AirPort facility on your computer, which enables you to perform wireless networking

- AirPort Setup Assistant. This sets up the AirPort wireless networking facility

- Audio MIDI Setup. This can be used for adding audio devices and setting their properties

- Bluetooth File Exchange. This determines how files are exchanged between your computer and other Bluetooth devices (if this function is enabled)

- ColorSysc Utility. This can be used to view and create color profiles on your computer. These can then be used by programs to try and match output color with the color that is displayed on the monitor

- Console. This displays the behind-the-scenes messages that are being passed around the computer while its usual tasks are being performed

- DigitalColor Meter. This can be used to measure the exact color values of a particular color

- Directory Access. This is an administration function for a network administrator. It allows them to give users access to various network services

- Disk Utility. This can be used to view information about attached disks and repair errors

- Grab. This is a utility which can be used to capture screen shots. These are images of the screen at a given point in time. You can grab different portions of the screen and even menus. The resultant images can be saved into different file formats

- Grapher. This is a utility for creating simple or more complex scientific graphs

Don't forget

You may never need to use a utility like the Console, but it is worth having a look at it just to see the inner workings of a computer.

Hot tip

The Grab utility is invaluable if you are producing manuals or books and need to display examples of a screen or program.

- Java folder. This is a folder that contains utilities that can be used to run and work with Java programs. It has specific utilities for Input Method Hotkey, Java Preferences and Java Web Start

- Keychain Access. This deals with items such as passwords when they are needed for networking. These do not have to be set but it can save time if you have to enter passwords on a lot of occasions. It also ensures that there is greater security for items protected by passwords

- Migration Assistant. This helps in the transfer of files between two Mac computers

- Network Utility. This is a problem determination guide to see if the problem is on the workstation or the network

- ODBC Administrator. This can be used to work with databases that are ODBC (Object Database Connectivity) compliant. It can access multiple databases from a single application

- Print Setup Utility. This is used to add and configure printers and to view the status of any current print jobs

- System Profiler. This contains details of the hardware devices and software applications that are installed on your computer (see Chapter Ten for more details)

- Terminal. This is used as an entry point into the world of UNIX. Within the Terminal you can view the workings of UNIX and also start to write your own programs, if you have some UNIX programming knowledge

- VoiceOver Utility. This has various options for how the VoiceOver function works within OS X. This is the digital voice that can be used to read out what is on the screen and it is particularly useful for users who are visually impaired

Printing

OS X Leopard makes the printing process as simple as possible, partly by being able to automatically instal new printers as soon as they are connected to your Mac. However, it is also possible to instal printers manually. To do this:

1 Open the System Preferences folder and then click on the Print & Fax button

2 Currently installed printers are displayed in the Printers List. Click here to add a new printer and follow the on-screen prompts

Don't forget

For most printers, OS X will detect them when they are first connected and they should be ready to use immediately without the need to instal any software or apply new settings.

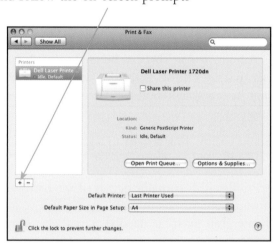

3 Once a printer has been installed (either automatically or manually) documents can be printed by selecting File>Print from the Menu bar. Print settings can be set at this point (see below) and they can also be set by selecting File>Page/Print Setup from the Menu bar in most programs

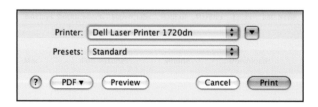

Creating PDF documents

PDF (Portable Document Format) is a file format that preserves the formatting of the original document and it can be viewed on a variety of computer platforms including Mac, Windows and UNIX. OS X has a built-in PDF function that can produce PDF files from most programs. To do this:

1 Open a file in any program and select File>Print from the Menu bar. Click on the PDF button

Don't forget

PDF files can be viewed with the Preview program within the Applications folder.

2 Browse to a destination for the file and click Save

3 Look in the selected location to view the newly created PDF file

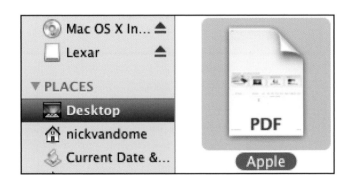

Hot tip

PDF is an excellent option if you are creating documents such as instruction booklets, magazines or manuals.

Faxing documents

With OS X you can fax any document as long as you have an internal or an external modem connected to your Mac. To do this:

1 Open the System Preferences folder and then click on the Print & Fax button

Print & Fax

2 If a modem is connected the Fax connection should appear here

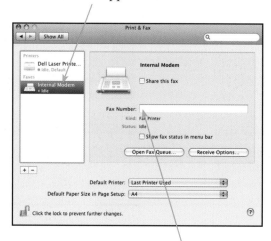

3 Enter a fax number and prefix here

4 Click on the Receive Options button to specify settings for incoming faxes

Receive Options...

5 Enter the required details and click on the OK button

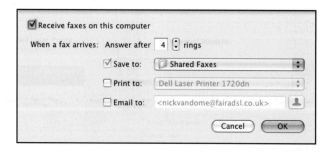

6 Internet and email

This chapter shows how to get the most out of the Internet and email. It covers connecting to the Internet and how to use the OS X Web browser, Safari and its email program, Mail. It also covers text and video chatting and the use of RSS news feeds.

Getting connected

Access to the Internet is an accepted part of the computing world and it is unusual for users not to want to do this. Not only does this provide a gateway to the World Wide Web but also email.

Connecting to the Internet with a Mac is done through the System Preferences. To do this:

Don't forget

Before you connect to the Internet you have to have an Internet Service Provider (ISP) who will provide you with the relevant method of connection, i.e. dial-up, cable or broadband. They will provide you with any login details.

1 Click on the System Preferences icon on the Dock

2 Click on the Network icon

3 Check that your method of connecting to the Internet is active, i.e. colored green

4 Click on the Assist me button to access wizards for connecting to the Internet with your preferred method of connection

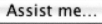

5 Click on the Assistant button Assistant...

6 The Network Setup Assistant is used to configure your
system so that you can connect to the Internet

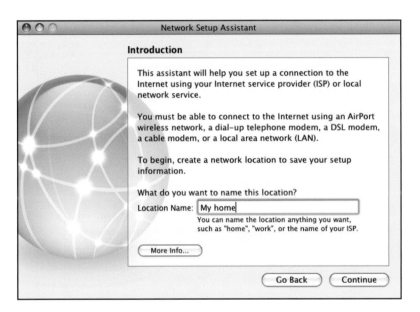

7 Enter a name for your connection

8 Click on the Continue button Continue

...cont'd

9 Select an option for how you will connect to the Internet, e.g. wireless, cable or telephone modem

10 Click on the Continue button

11 For a wireless connection, select an available wireless network. This will be the router that is being used to make the connection

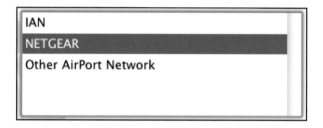

12 Enter a password for the router (this will have been created when you connected and configured the router)

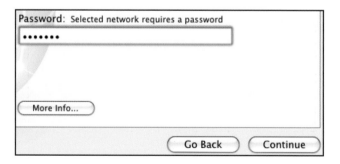

13 Click on the Continue button

14 The Ready to Connect window informs you that you are about to attempt to connect to your network

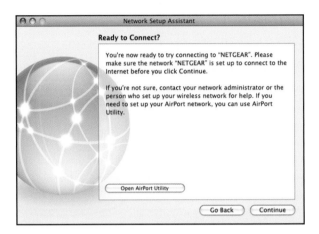

15 Click on the Continue button

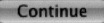

16 You are informed if the connection has been successful

17 Click on the Done button

Safari

Safari is a Web browser that is designed specifically to be used with OS X. It is similar in most respects to other browsers, but it usually functions more quickly and works seamlessly with OS X.

Safari overview

1 Click here on the Dock to launch Safari

Hot tip

If the Address Bar is not visible, select View from the Menu bar and check on the Address Bar option. From this menu you can also select or deselect items such as the Back/Forward buttons and the Stop/Reload buttons.

Back and forward   Refresh   Address bar   Search

Bookmarks bar

Page content

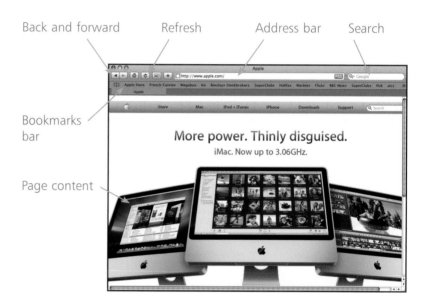

2 Select Safari>Preferences from the Menu bar to specify settings for the way Safari operates and displays Web pages

Adding bookmarks

Bookmarks are a device by which you can create quick links to your favorite Web pages or the ones you visit most frequently. Bookmarks can be added to a menu or the Bookmarks bar in Safari which makes them even quicker to access. Folders can also be created to store the less frequently used bookmarks. To view and create bookmarks:

Beware

Only keep your most frequently used bookmarks in the Bookmarks Bar. Otherwise some of them will cease to be visible, as there will be too many entries for the available space.

1 Click here to view all bookmarks

2 All of the saved bookmarks are displayed in the Bookmarks window

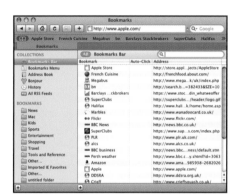

Hot tip

If you are registered for the .Mac service, you can upload all of your bookmarks to your online account and you will be able to access them from any computer with an Internet connection.

3 Click here to create a bookmark for the page currently being viewed

4 Enter a name for the bookmark and select a location in which to store it

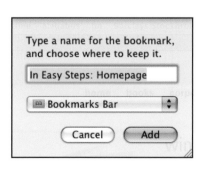

Type a name for the bookmark, and choose where to keep it.

In Easy Steps: Homepage

Bookmarks Bar

Cancel   Add

5 Click on the Add button

117

Safari RSS

RSS, which stands for Really Simple Syndication, is a method of producing regularly updated information on websites. It works by using XML (Extensible Markup Language) and is most frequently seen on news websites: the RSS feed displays the latest news. In order for a RSS feed to be viewed, the browser has to support the RSS technology. Safari does this and when it comes across a website with RSS this icon is displayed in the Safari address bar:

Once an RSS enabled site has been located the news feeds can be accessed by clicking on the RSS icon.

RSS preferences

The way that RSS feeds are dealt with can be set within the Safari preferences by selecting Safari>Preferences from the Menu bar:

Don't forget

RSS is becoming increasingly popular and more and more websites are now using it for areas such as news.

1 Click here to access RSS settings

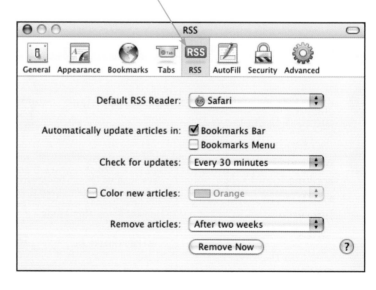

2 Specific settings can be made in the RSS window

Mail

Email is an essential element for most computer users and Macs come with their own email program called Mail. This covers all of the email functionality that anyone could need.

When first using Mail you have to set up your email account. This information will be available from the company who provides your email service, although in some cases Mail may obtain this information automatically. To view your Mail account details:

1 Click on this icon on the Dock

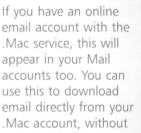

2 Select Mail>Preferences from the Menu bar

3 Click on the Accounts tab

4 If it has not already been included, enter the details of your email account in the Account Information section

5 Click on this button to close the Mail Preferences window

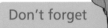
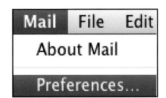

119

Adding mailboxes

Before you start creating email messages it is a good idea to create a folder structure (mailboxes) for your emails. This will allow you to sort your emails into relevant subjects when you receive them, rather than having all of them sitting in your Inbox. To add a structure of new mailboxes:

1 Mailboxes are displayed in the Mailboxes panel

120

2 At the bottom of the Mailboxes panel, click on this icon

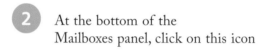

3 Select where you want the mailbox to be created (by default this will be On My Mac)

4 Enter a name for the new mailbox

5 Click on the OK button

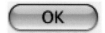

6 The new mailbox is added to the current list

Creating email

Mail enables you to send and receive emails and also format them to your own style. This can be simply formatting text or adding customized stationery.

To access Mail and start creating email messages:

1   Click on this icon on the Dock

2   Mail contains options for creating, receiving and formatting email messages

3   Click on this button to create a new email message

4   Enter the email address of the recipient in the To box

To: robin.vandome@mac.com

5   Enter a title for the email in the Subject box

Subject: Well done

Hot tip

If you Forward an email with an attachment then the attachment is included. If you Reply to an email the attachment will not be included.

Hot tip

When entering the name of a recipient for a message, Mail will display details of matching names from your Address Book. For instance, if you type DA, all of the entries in your Address Book beginning with this will be displayed and you can select the required one.

...cont'd

6 Enter the content for the email here

7 To format the text in the email, select it first

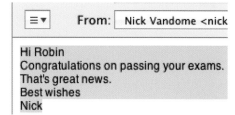

8 Click on the Fonts button

9 Select formatting options for the text

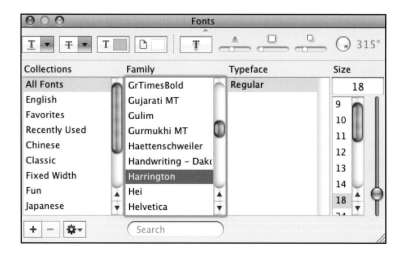

10 Click on the Send button to send the email to the selected recipient

Dealing with junk email

Spam, or junk email, is the scourge of every email user. It is unwanted and unsolicited messages that are usually sent in bulk to lists of email addresses. In Mail there is a function to try and limit the amount of junk email that you receive in your Inbox. To do this:

1 When you receive a junk email, click on this button on the Mail toolbar (initially this will help to train Mail to identify junk email)

2 Once Mail has recognized the types of junk that you receive it will start to filter them directly into the Junk Mailbox

Hot tip

It is worth occasionally checking in your Junk Mailbox, in case something you want has been put there.

123

3 To set the preferences for junk email select Mail>Preferences from the Menu bar and click on the Junk tab

4 Junk email is displayed in the Junk Mailbox

●	💬	From	Subject
○		WebProNews	If They're Searching, Give ...
●		Maricela Goddard	Let yourself look really swell!

Attaching photos

Emails do not have to be restricted to plain text. Through the use of attachments they can also include other documents and particularly photos. This is an excellent way to send photos to family and friends around the world. There are two ways to attach photos to an email:

Attach button
To attach photos using the Attach button:

1 Click on this icon on the Mail toolbar

124

2 Browse your hard drive for the photo(s) you want to include in your email. Select the photos you want

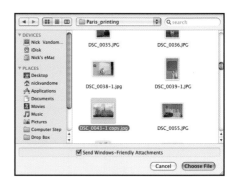

3 Click on the Choose File button

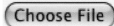

4 The photo is added to the body of the email

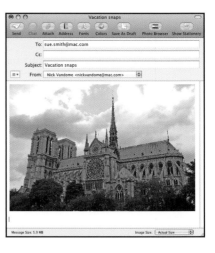

Photo Browser

To attach photos using the Photo Browser:

1 Click on this icon on the Mail toolbar

2 Browse the Photo Browser for the photo(s) that you want to include

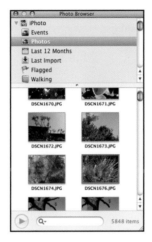

The Photo Browser is available from a variety of other applications.

3 Drag the selected photo(s) into the open email to include them in the message

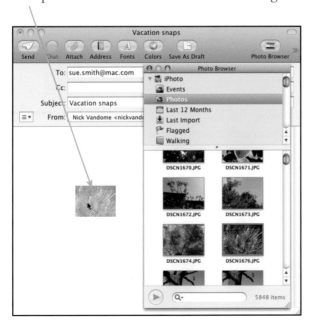

Email stationery

You do not have to settle for conservative formatting options in emails and Mail offers a variety of templates that can give your messages a creative and eye-catching appearance. It can also be used to format any photos that you have attached to your message. This is done through the use of the Stationery function within Mail. To use this:

1 Click on this icon on the Mail toolbar

2 Select a category for the stationery

3 Double-click on a style to apply it to the email

4 The stationery incorporates any photos that have been attached to the email

iChat

One issue with email is that you can never be sure when the recipient receives the message, or when they will reply to it. For a more immediate form of communication, instant messaging or video messaging can be used. This is done with the iChat program. To use this:

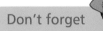

Don't forget

If a buddy has a green circle next to their name, it means that they are currently online and available for chatting.

1 Click on this icon on the Dock

2 In order to chat to someone you have to add them as a buddy. To do this, click on this button:

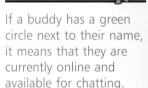

Don't forget

Preferences for how iChat operates can be chosen by selecting iChat>Preferences from the Menu bar.

3 Enter the required details in the buddy window and click on the Add button

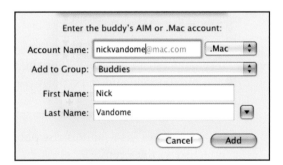

Don't forget

To use iChat you have to have a .Mac (or AOL) account activated.

4 Select a buddy in the iChat window

5 Click on this button to start a text chat

6 Click on this button to start a video chat

iChat AV

iChat AV operates in the same way as iChat, except that it uses video for communication rather than text. To use iChat AV you require a cable or broadband Internet connection and the iSight video camera, that can be attached to any Mac. To use iChat AV:

1 Open iChat and select a buddy

2 Click here to invite the buddy to a video chat

3 Click here to view your own video screen

4 Before the video chat starts your image appears here. Once the chat starts this is minimized, but still visible, and the other person's image takes up the main part of the screen

5 Click here to select preferences for the way iChat AV operates

6 Preferences can be selected for the type of camera used, the microphone and the type of connection

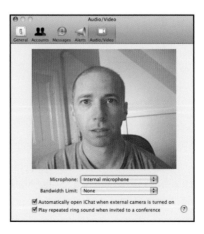

128

7 Using .Mac

This chapter shows how the online .Mac service can be used to expand your OS X horizons and participate in a genuine joined-up digital world by sharing your files and also your experiences. It looks at the most valuable .Mac features.

Sharing with .Mac

Some companies make computers and some companies run online services for email and sharing files. However, Apple does both: their .Mac online sharing service is closely integrated so that sharing items online is virtually the same as working with them on your Mac computer. There is an annual subscription fee for .Mac but for this you get:

- An online email account that you can synchronize with your Mac computer

- An online version of your Mac Address Book

- An option for creating your own website

- Online greeting cards

- Online disk space for storage or backing up

- Bookmarks that you have set up on your Mac

- Groups to which you can invite friends and family members

To join .Mac and start using its services:

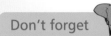

Don't forget

.Mac probably contains all of the services you will need for interacting online.

1 Go to the .Mac homepage at www.apple.com/dotmac/

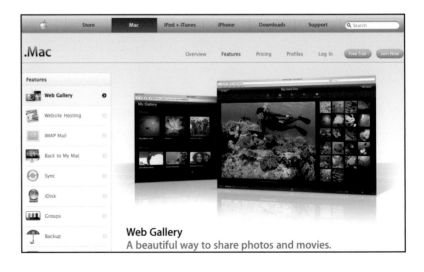

Web Gallery
A beautiful way to share photos and movies.

2 Click on the Free Trial or the Join Now button

3 For both options in Step 2 you will have to register. The Free Trial is for 60 days, while the normal sign up involves paying the annual subscription fee

---

🌐 **.mac**   Sign up for a 60 day free trial

To sign up for your free trial, please provide the following information and click Continue.

Personal Information

First Name   Last Name

Current Email Address

Country   Language
United States   English

Member Name and Password

Choose a Member Name (3-20 characters)   Password (6-32 characters)
                              @mac.com

Your member name will also be your email name and   Password (confirm)
cannot be changed after sign-up.

Don't forget

Once you have subscribed to the full .Mac service your subscription will be debited automatically each year unless you specify for it to stop. You will receive an email about a month before, telling you the date of the next payment.

131

4 Once you have registered, click on the Mail button to access your online email

Mail   0 ✉

5 Once you are signed up for .Mac this email account will be available on your Mac computer too. The .Mac email enables you to access your email from any Internet enabled computer in the world

Creating an iDisk

iDisk is a function of .Mac that effectively enables you to have a backup hard drive online. The basic .Mac membership gives you 10 Gb of storage on your iDisk.

iDisk can be used to back up your files and it is possible to access files on iDisk from any Internet enabled computer. To use iDisk:

1 When you register for .Mac the iDisk icon will appear in the Finder

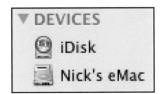

2 Select a file or folder that you want to include on your iDisk

3 Select File>Copy from the Finder Menu bar

4 Double-click on the iDisk icon and locate a folder into which you want to place the file or folder

5 Select File>Paste from the Finder Menu bar

6 Once you have added files or folders to your iDisk icon in the Finder these will automatically be copied to your online iDisk on .Mac (as long as you have an active Internet connection)

Viewing your iDisk online

To view the contents of your iDisk from within .Mac:

1 Access the .Mac homepage and log in to your account

2 In the .Mac panel scroll down until you see the iDisk icon. Click on it

3 The contents of your iDisk are displayed. Double-click on a folder to display its contents

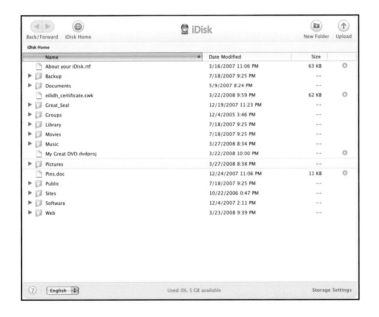

4 Click on this icon next to a file to download it onto whichever computer you are accessing it from

133

iDisk preferences

Within the System Preferences folder it is possible to determine how iDisk works on your Mac. To do this:

1 Click on the System Preferences icon on the Dock

2 In the System Preferences folder, click on the .Mac icon

3 Click on the iDisk tab

4 This scale shows how much iDisk space you have used up

5 Click on the Upgrade Storage button to go online to purchase more iDisk space from .Mac

Upgrade Storage...

Beware

If you allow Read and Write access to your iDisk Public Folder this means that other people will be able to access and edit the files contained in this folder.

6 Select how you want other people to be able to access your Public Folder within iDisk

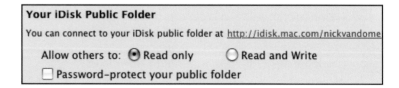

Synchronizing with .Mac

One of the potential problems with having copies of the same files on your computer and on the .Mac site is that there is the potential for them to become unsynchronized if you update one version and not the other. This is overcome by the synchronization function which ensures that the relevant information on your computer and your .Mac account are both synchronized. This means that wherever you access your .Mac account from you can be sure that it is the same information as on your Mac computer. To do this:

1 Click on the System Preferences icon on the Dock

2 Click on the .Mac icon (as on the previous page)

3 Click on the Sync tab

4 Check on the items you want synchronized

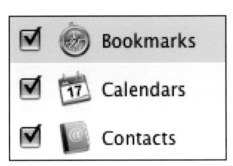

Don't forget

If there is a conflict between your Mac and your .Mac account you will be alerted to the fact and asked how you would like to resolve it.

5 Check on this box to have your Mac computer and .Mac account synchronized automatically

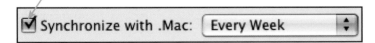

6 Click on the Sync Now button

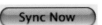

Web Gallery

.Mac is a great environment in which to share your photos and videos online. This is done by uploading them into a Web Gallery in your .Mac account. You can then invite family and friends to come and view them. To do this:

1 Click on the iPhoto icon on the Dock

2 In iPhoto select the photos you want to use in the Web Gallery

3 Click on the Web Gallery button

4 Set preferences for how you would like people to view and use your Web Gallery

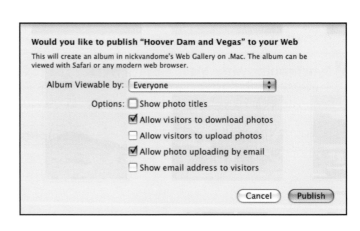

Would you like to publish "Hoover Dam and Vegas" to your Web

This will create an album in nickvandome's Web Gallery on .Mac. The album can be viewed with Safari or any modern web browser.

Album Viewable by: [Everyone ▲]

Options: ☐ Show photo titles
☑ Allow visitors to download photos
☐ Allow visitors to upload photos
☑ Allow photo uploading by email
☐ Show email address to visitors

(Cancel) (Publish)

5 Click on the Publish button

6 Click on the link at the top of the iPhoto window to go to your .Mac Web Gallery

Hoover Dam and Vegas
http://gallery.mac.com/nickvandome/100016 ○

7 The Web Gallery is published within your .Mac account

8 Click on the Tell a Friend button to invite other people to view your Web Gallery

...cont'd

9 Enter your email address

From: nickvandome@mac.com

10 Enter the recipient's email address

To: brianjones@mac.com

11 Enter a message

Message: Hi Brian
Here are some photos from our recent trip to
Vegas and the Hoover Dam. Great!

Don't forget

The visible code is
needed to ensure that
there are not bulk, or
automated submissions
to this service on .Mac.

12 Enter the visible code

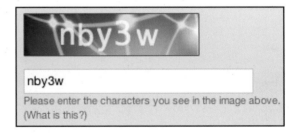

nby3w

Please enter the characters you see in the image above.
(What is this?)

13 Click on the Send button

Send

Viewing a Web Gallery

When you invite someone to view one of your Web Galleries they receive an email with the following message:

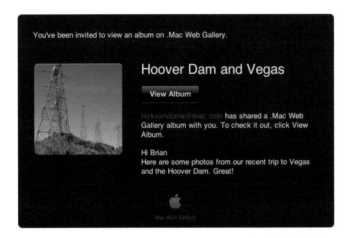

When they click on the View Album button they will be taken straight to the appropriate Gallery:

139

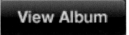

Hot tip

Images can be viewed at different sizes in a Web Gallery by dragging the slider in the bottom right-hand corner of the Web Gallery window.

.Mac Mail

When you register for .Mac you are automatically assigned an online email account. This account can also be accessed from your Mac account using the Mail program. In this way you can have a fully synchronized email account that you can use online and also on your desktop Mac or laptop. To access and use Mail with your .Mac account:

1 Log in to your .Mac account and click on the Mail link

2 The .Mac interface is similar to the one that appears on your Mac when you access your email

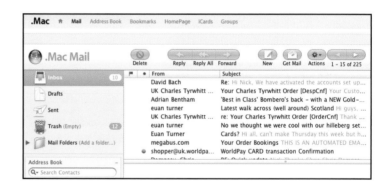

Don't forget

If your .Mac account is synchronized with your OS X Address Book then this will be available within your .Mac Mail account, using the Address button.

3 Click on the New button to create a new email

4 Click on the Address button to access names from your online address book

Creating a group

Groups on .Mac are collaborative areas where groups of people can view and share files. To join a group you have to have a .Mac ID, although you do not have to still be an active .Mac member. To create a group:

1 Log in to your .Mac account and click on the Groups link

2 Click on the Create a New Group button

3 Enter details for the Group

Don't forget

Photos can be added to a group and a group discussion can also be undertaken.

4 Click on the Submit button

5 Access your Group in your .Mac account

Nick's test
http://groups.mac.com/nickv1

 Owner   Edit

6 Within the Members' area, click on the Invite link to invite new members

Members

Search   [   ]

Nick Vandome

Invite or Manage

Backup

Backup is a program that can be downloaded from .Mac and then used to back up files to your iDisk, so that they are saved in an online environment. To do this:

1 Download Backup from your .Mac account

2 Click on the Backup icon on the Dock or access it in the Applications folder

Backup

3 Select to back up your files to your iDisk

Back up to iDisk

4 Check on the items you want included in the backup

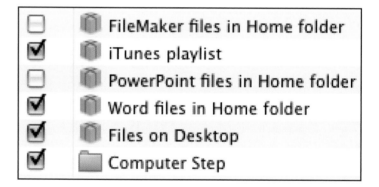

- ☐ FileMaker files in Home folder
- ☑ iTunes playlist
- ☐ PowerPoint files in Home folder
- ☑ Word files in Home folder
- ☑ Files on Desktop
- ☑ Computer Step

5 Click on this button to add other items to the backup

6 Click on this button to select options for your backup to be performed automatically

7 Click on the Backup Now button to start the backup

Backup Now

8 Sharing OS X

This chapter looks at how to set up different user accounts and how to keep everyone safe on your Mac using parental controls.

Adding users

OS X enables multiple users to access individual accounts on the same computer. If there are multiple users, i.e. two or more, for a single machine, each person can sign on individually and access their own files and folders. This means that each person can log in to their own settings and preferences. All user accounts can be password protected, to ensure that each user's environment is secure. To set up multiple user accounts:

1   Click on the System Preferences icon on the Dock

2   Click on the Accounts icon

3   The information about the current account is displayed. This is your own account and the information is based on details you provide when you first set up your Mac

4   Click on this icon to enable new accounts to be added (the padlock needs to be open)

5 Click on the plus sign icon to add a new account

6 Enter the details for the new account holder

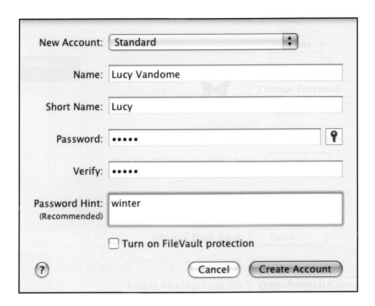

New Account:	Standard ⬦
Name:	Lucy Vandome
Short Name:	Lucy
Password:	••••• 🔑
Verify:	•••••
Password Hint: (Recommended)	winter

☐ Turn on FileVault protection

(?) (Cancel) (Create Account)

Don't forget

By default, you are the administrator of your own Mac. This means that you can administer other user accounts.

7 Click on the Create Account button

Create Account

8 The new account is added to the list in the Accounts window, under Other Accounts

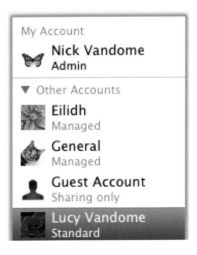

My Account

Nick Vandome
Admin

▼ Other Accounts

Eilidh
Managed

General
Managed

Guest Account
Sharing only

Lucy Vandome
Standard

Hot tip

If an administrator forgets their password, insert the OS X CD while holding down the C key. Once this opens, select Installer>Reset Password from the Menu bar. Then select the correct user and enter a new password. Click on Save to apply the changes.

Deleting users

Once a user has been added, their name appears on the list in the Accounts preference dialog box. It is then possible to edit the details of a particular user or delete them altogether. To do this:

1 Select a user from the list

2 Click here to remove the selected person's user account

3 A warning box appears to check if you really do want to delete the selected user. If you do, select the required option and click on OK

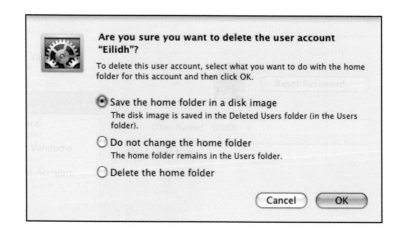

Fast user switching

If there are multiple users using OS X it is useful to be able to switch between them as quickly as possible. When this is done, the first user's session is retained so that they can return to it if required. To switch between users:

1 In the Accounts window, click on the Login Options button

2 Check on the Enable Fast User Switching box

3 At the top-right of the screen, click on the current user's name

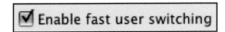

4 Click on the name of another user

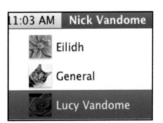

5 Enter the relevant password (if required)

6 Click on the Log In button

Don't forget

When you switch between users, the first user remains logged in and their current session is retained intact.

147

Viewing user accounts

It is possible for individual users to see the overview of another user's account. They can also exchange files with other users by placing them in a folder called a Drop Box. This means that the user can then access these files the next time they log in to their own account. (Under normal circumstances they would not be able to view any folders or files in someone else's account). To view another user's folders and share files in the Finder:

148

1 Select the hard drive and double-click on the Users folder

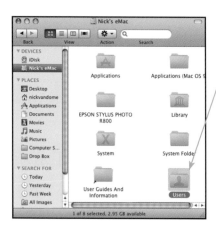

2 Double-click on another user's folder to view its contents

3 Folders with a No Entry icon indicate that they cannot be accessed

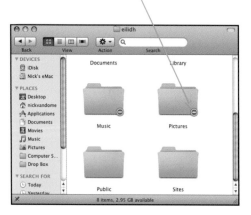

OS X for the family

Many families share their computers between multiple users and with the ability to create different accounts in OS X each user can have their own customized workspace. However, if children are using the computer parents may want to restrict access to certain types of information that can be viewed, particularly in relation to the Internet and email. Controls can be set within the Accounts system preference. To do this:

1 Access the user Accounts as shown on page 144

2 Click on a username and check on the Enable Parental Controls box and click on the Open Parental Controls button to access the Parental Controls

Hot tip

To check which sites have been viewed on a Web browser, check the History menu, which is located on the main Menu bar.

System controls

1 Click on the System tab

2 Check on the Use Simple Finder box to show a simplified version of the Finder

☑ Use Simple Finder
Provides a simplified view of the computer desktop for young or inexperienced users.

3 Check on this box if you want to limit the types of program that a user can access

☑ Only allow selected applications
Allows user to open only the selected applications. An administrator's password is required to open other applications.

4 Check off the boxes next to the programs that you do not want used

Check the applications to allow

▶ ☐ iLife
▶ ☑ iWork
▼ ☐ Internet
   ☐ Explorer
   ☐ iChat
   ☑ Mail
   ☑ Safari

...cont'd

Content controls

1 Click on the Content tab

2 Check on this box to prevent any profanities in the Mac Dictionary being displayed

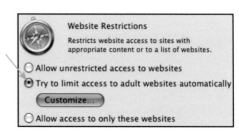

3 Check on this button and click on the Customize button to edit the type of Web content that can be viewed

4 Enter the Web addresses for sites that are acceptable

Always allow these sites:
http://www.ineasysteps.com

5 Enter the Web addresses for sites that are not acceptable

Never allow these sites:
http://www.badcontent.com

Mail and iChat controls

1 Click on the Mail & iChat tab

Mail & iChat

2 Check on the Limit boxes to limit the type of content in email messages and iChat text messages

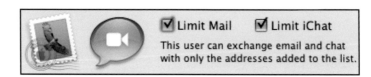

Time Limits controls

1 Click on the Time Limits tab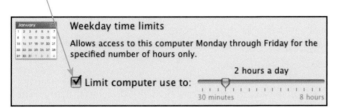

2 Check on this box to limit the amount of time the user can use the Mac

Weekday time limits

Allows access to this computer Monday through Friday for the specified number of hours only.

2 hours a day

☑ Limit computer use to:

30 minutes   8 hours

3 Check on these boxes to determine the times at which the user cannot access their account

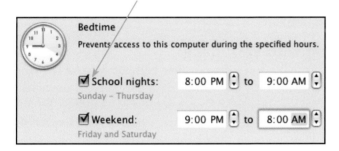

Bedtime

Prevents access to this computer during the specified hours.

☑ School nights: 8:00 PM ⬍ to   9:00 AM ⬍

Sunday – Thursday

☑ Weekend: 9:00 PM ⬍ to   8:00 AM ⬍

Friday and Saturday

Log controls

1 Click on the Logs tab   **Logs**

2 The logs can be edited to show activity over a certain time period and content type

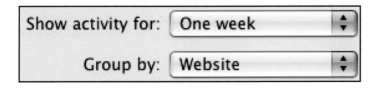

Show activity for: One week

Group by: Website

OS X for Windows users

General sharing

One of the historical complaints about Macs is that it is difficult to share files between them and Microsoft Windows computers. While this may have been true with some file types in years gone by, this is an issue that is becoming less and less important, particularly with OS X. Some of the reasons for this are:

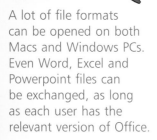

- A number of popular file formats, such as PDFs (Portable Document Format) for documents and JPEGs (Joint Photographic Experts Group) for photos and images, are designed so that they can be used on both Mac and Windows platforms

- A lot of software programs on the Mac have options for saving files into different formats, including ones that are specifically for Windows machines

- Other popular programs, such as Microsoft Office, now have Mac versions and the resulting files can be shared on both formats

Sharing with Boot Camp

For people who find it hard to live without Microsoft Windows, help is at hand even on a Mac. Macs have a program called Boot Camp that can be used to run a version of Windows on a Mac. This is only available with Leopard. Once it has been accessed, a copy of Windows can then be installed and run. This means that if you have a non-Mac program that you want to use on your Mac, you can do so with Boot Camp.

Boot Camp is set up with the Boot Camp Assistant which is located within the Utilities folder within the Applications folder. Once this is run you can then install either Windows XP or Vista which will run at its native speed. If you need drivers for specific programs these can be obtained from your Leopard installation disc.

9 Advanced features

This chapter looks at some of the more advanced capabilities of OS X such as the programming language AppleScript, the Automator and also how to create a network and share files over a network.

AppleScript

AppleScript is a programming language which can be used to write your own programs to run with OS X. These can be complex applications or they could be simple utility programs. In addition to writing your own AppleScript, OS X also comes bundled with various scripts that have already been created. These can then be used on your Mac computer. To access the AppleScript options:

Don't forget

Even for non-programmers, AppleScript is a viable option for creating simple programs within OS X.

1 In the Applications folder, double-click on the AppleScript folder

Hot tip

A good way to gain a general understanding of AppleScript is to look at some of the scripts in the Example Scripts folder and then open them in Script Editor (double-click on the script name in the Example Scripts folder to open it in Script Editor). This will enable you to see how the scripts are created and the syntax they use.

2 The available AppleScript options are available in the folder

Launching scripts

To launch existing AppleScripts:

1 Double-click on the Example Scripts folder

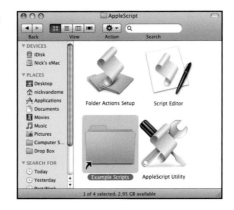

2 Double-click on a script folder

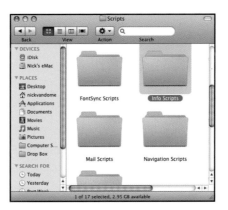

Don't forget

Some AppleScripts are more useful than others. Experiment with different ones to see which best fit your own needs.

3 Double-click on a script to open it

...cont'd

④ The script is displayed in the Script Editor

⑤ Click on the Run button to execute the script

⑥ Once the script has been run, the results are displayed in the relevant application, according to the type of script

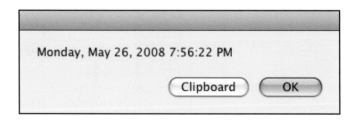

Writing scripts

If you have some programming knowledge you may want to create your own AppleScripts. To do this:

1 Open the AppleScript folder and double-click on the Script Editor

2 Write the required AppleScript. At this point it will look like unformatted text

Don't forget

For more information about AppleScript, have a look on the Apple website at www.apple.com/applescript/

3 Click on the Compile button. This will check the syntax of the script and format it according to the items that have been entered, as above

```
tell application "Finder"
    activate
    say "Hello Nick, how are you today?"
    open application "iPhoto"
    open application "iCal"
end tell
```

...cont'd

4 If there is a problem with the script, the Compiler will display an error message. Click OK to return to the script and correct the syntax error

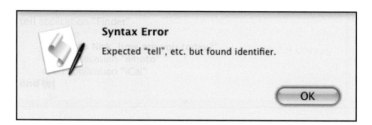

Syntax Error

Expected "tell", etc. but found identifier.

OK

5 Select File>Save from the Menu bar. Select either Script or Application as the file format

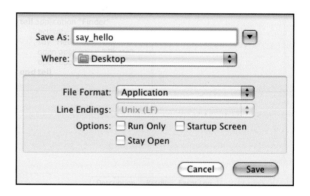

Save As: say_hello

Where: Desktop

File Format: Application

Line Endings: Unix (LF)

Options: ☐ Run Only   ☐ Startup Screen
☐ Stay Open

Cancel   Save

6 Click on the Save button

7 Scripts are denoted by this icon

8 Applications are denoted by this icon

say_hello

say_hello

Using scripts

Once scripts have been created and saved they can either be run manually or automatically.

Using scripts manually
Save the script as an application and double-click on it in its folder or add it to the Finder Sidebar and single click on it here

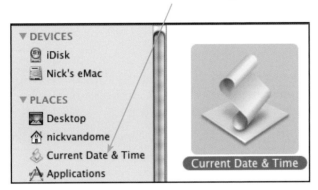

Using scripts automatically

Depending on how a script has been saved as an application a dialog box may appear asking you to Run the application in order to execute it.

1 Open System Preferences and select the Accounts preference. Click on the Login Items tab and click on the Plus button

2 Browse to the required script and select it

3 Click on the Add button to include it in the startup process. The script will then run when the computer is booted up

Automator

Automator is an OS X application that can be used to automate a series of repetitive tasks, such as renaming a folder full of images. It works by creating a workflow of tasks, which can then be applied to a specified list of folders or files. There are numerous Automator functions that are included with the application and developers are adding more constantly. To create a new workflow in Automator:

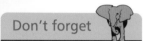

New Automator workflows can be downloaded from the Apple website at: www.apple.com

1 Double-click on this icon in the Applications folder or click on it once if it has been added to the Dock

2 This left-hand panel contains details of applications to which certain Automator actions can be applied. Click on one to show its actions

3 Select files to which you want an Automator action applied

Don't forget

Numerous actions can be added to a single workflow. However, make sure that you want all of the actions to be applied to all of the selected files or folders.

4 Drag the selected files into the right-hand Automator panel

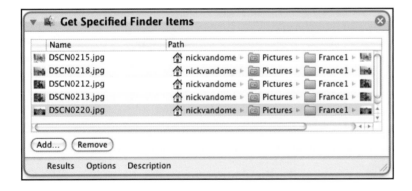

5 Click on the Add button

...cont'd

6 Click here to set the specific criteria for an action within the workflow

Mail	Create Thumbnail Images
Movies	Crop Images
Music	Download Pictures
PDFs	Filter iPhoto Items
Photos	Find iPhoto Items

Beware

Depending on the processes involved and the number of steps, it can take a few minutes to execute an Automator workflow.

7 The selected action is entered below the selected files

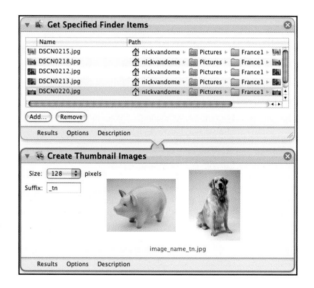

8 Click on the Run button to run the workflow, i.e. have it applied to the selected folders or images

9 The completed workflow is indicated here

10 Click on the Results button to view the results within the Automator window

Hot tip

Automator workflows can also be created by first selecting the required folders or files, then Ctrl+click and selecting Automator from the menu.

11 View the source files to check that the workflow has been applied as expected

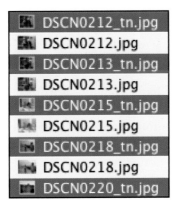

12 Once the workflow has been completed, select File>Save from the Automator Menu bar to save it. This will keep it for future use

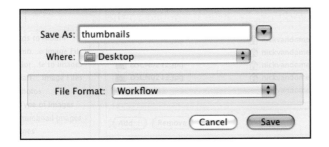

Networking overview

Before you start sharing files directly between computers, you have to connect them together. This is known as networking and can be done with two computers in the same room, or with thousands of computers in a major corporation. If you are setting up your own small network it will be known in the computing world as a Local Area Network (LAN). When setting up a network there are various pieces of hardware that are initially required to join all of the required items together. Once this has been done, software settings can be applied for the networked items. Some of the items of hardware that may be required include:

- A network card. This is known as a Network Interface Card (NIC) and all recent Macs have them built-in

- An Ethernet port and Ethernet cable. This enables you to make the physical connection between devices. Ethernet cables come in a variety of forms but the one you should be looking for is the Cat5E type as this allows for the fastest transfer of data. If you are creating a wireless network then you will not require these

- A hub. This is a piece of hardware with multiple Ethernet ports that enables you to connect all of your devices together and let them communicate with each other. However, conflicts can occur with hubs if two devices try and send data through it at the same time

- A switch. This is similar in operation to a hub but it is more sophisticated in its method of data transfer, thus allowing all of the machines on the network to communicate simultaneously, unlike a hub

Once you have worked out all of the devices that you want to include on your network you can arrange them accordingly. Try and keep the switches and hub within relative proximity of a power supply and, if you are using cables, make sure they are laid out safely.

It is perfectly possible to create a simple network of two computers by joining them with an Ethernet cable.

Hot tip

If you have two Macs to be networked and they are in close proximity then this can be achieved with an Ethernet crossover cable. If you have more than two computers, then this is where an Ethernet hub is required. In both cases, there is no need to connect to the Internet to achieve the network.

Ethernet network

The cheapest and easiest way to network computers is to create an Ethernet network. This involves buying an Ethernet hub or switch, which enables you to connect several devices to a central point, i.e. the hub or switch. All Apple computers and most modern printers have an Ethernet connection, so it is possible to connect various devices, not just computers. Once all of the devices have been connected by Ethernet cables, you can then start applying network settings.

AirPort network

The other option for creating a network is an AirPort network. This is a wireless network and there are two main standards used by Apple computers: AirPort, using the IEEE 802.11b standard, which is more commonly known as Wi-Fi, which stands for Wireless Fidelity and the newer AirPort Extreme, using the newer IEEE 802.11g standard which is up to 5 times faster than the older 802.11b standard. Thankfully AirPort Extreme is also compatible with devices based on the older standard, so one machine loaded with AirPort Extreme can still communicate wirelessly with an older AirPort one.

One of the issues with a wireless network is security since it is possible for someone with a wireless-enabled machine to access your wireless network, if they are within range. However, in the majority of cases the chances of this happening are fairly slim, although it is an issue about which you should be aware.

The basics of a wireless network with Macs is an AirPort card (either AirPort or AirPort Extreme) installed in all of the required machines and an AirPort base station that can be located anywhere within 150 metres of the AirPort enabled computers. Once the hardware is in place, wireless-enabled devices can be configured by using the AirPort Setup Assistant utility found in the Utilities folder. After AirPort has been set up the wireless network can be connected. All of the wireless-enabled devices should then be able to communicate with each other, without the use of a multitude of cables.

Don't forget

Another method for connecting items wirelessly is called Bluetooth. This covers much shorter distances than AirPort and is usually used for items such as printers and cellphones. Bluetooth devices can be connected by using the Bluetooth Setup Assistant in the Utilities folder.

Network settings

Once you have connected the hardware required for a network, you can start applying the network settings that are required for different computers to communicate with one another. To do this (the following example is for networking two Mac computers):

1 In System Preferences, double-click on the Network icon

2 For a wireless connection, click on the Airport button

3 Details of wireless settings are displayed

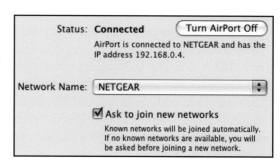

4 For a cable connection, click on the Ethernet button

5 Details of the cable settings are displayed

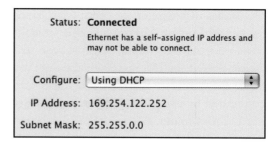

6 Click on the Advanced button to see the full settings for each option

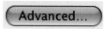

File sharing

One of the main reasons for creating a network of two or more computers is to share files between them. On networked Macs, this involves setting them up so that they can share files and then accessing these files.

Setting up file sharing

To set up file sharing on a networked Mac:

1 Click on the System Preference icon on the Dock

2 Click on the Sharing icon

Beware

If no file sharing options are enabled in the Sharing preference window, no other users will be able to access your computer or your files, even on a network.

3 Check on the boxes next to the items you want to share (the most common items to share are files and printers)

On	Service
☐	Screen Sharing
☑	File Sharing
☑	Printer Sharing
☐	Web Sharing
☐	Remote Login
☐	Remote Management
☐	Remote Apple Events
☐	Xgrid Sharing
☐	Internet Sharing

Hot tip

Networks can also be created between Macs and Windows-based PCs.

4 Click on the padlock to close it and prevent more changes

Connecting to a network

Connecting as a registered user

To connect as a registered user (usually as yourself when you want to access items on another one of your own computers):

1 Other connected computers on the network will show up in the Shared section in the Finder. Click on a networked computer

2 Click on the Connect As button

3 Check on the Registered User button and enter your username and password

4 Click on the Connect button

5 The hard drive and home folder of the networked computer are available to the registered user. Double-click on an item to view its contents

Guest users

Guest users on a network are users other than yourself, or other registered users, to whom you want to limit access to your files and folders. Guests only have access to a folder called the Drop Box in your own Public folder. To share files with Guest users you have to first copy them into the Drop Box. To do this:

1 Create a file and select File>Save from the Menu bar

2 Navigate to your own home folder (this is created automatically by OS X and displayed in the Finder Sidebar)

3 Double-click on the Public folder

4 Double-click on the Drop Box folder

5 Save the file into the Drop Box

Beware

If another user is having problems accessing the files in your Drop Box, check the permissions settings that have been assigned to the files. See Chapter Ten, page 186 for further details.

Hot tip

The contents of the Drop Box can be accessed by other users on the same computer as well as users on a network.

169

...cont'd

Accessing a Drop Box

To access files in a Drop Box:

1 Double-click on a networked computer in the Finder

2 Click on the Connect As button in the Finder window

3 Check on the Guest button

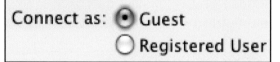

Beware

It is best to copy files into the Drop Box rather than moving them completely from their current location.

4 Click on the Connect button

5 Double-click on the administrator's home folder

nickvandome

Hot tip

Set permissions for how the Drop Box operates by selecting it in the Finder and Ctrl+clicking on it. Select Get Info from the menu and apply the required settings under the Ownership & Permissions heading.

6 Double-click on the Drop Box folder to access the files within it

Drop Box

Wireless networking

Networks can be created with computers connected with cables, but a more flexible method is to create a wireless network. This can be done with a wireless router and, using either an Airport or Airport Express base station, it can be done with a non-wireless router (i.e. a cable or DSL one) and wireless enabled Mac computers. Once the base station has been connected to the router it has to be configured so that the computers can recognize it. To do this:

1 Double-click the AirPort Setup Assistant icon in the Utilities folder

Don't forget

If a network card is installed in a Mac computer, it should be able to identify a new base station once it is plugged in.

2 The Airport Setup Assistant contains a Wizard that takes you through the setup process

3 Check on the Set up an Airport Base Station button

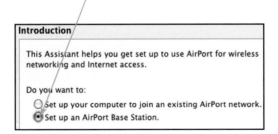

4 Click on the Continue button

...cont'd

5 Select any available Airport networks

| Available AirPort networks: | NETGEAR | ⬍ |

6 Click on the Continue button   [Continue]

7 Enter a password for the network (this will be the password used for the router when it was first configured)

The AirPort Network "NETGEAR" is protected by a password. Please enter the password.

Password: ••••••••

8 Click on the Continue button to complete the configuration   [Continue]

9 If you are trying to connect to a non-Airport base station the connection will fail and the following warning message will appear

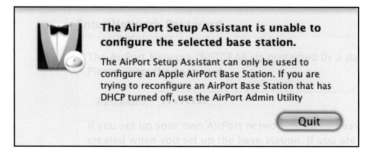

The AirPort Setup Assistant is unable to configure the selected base station.

The AirPort Setup Assistant can only be used to configure an Apple AirPort Base Station. If you are trying to reconfigure an AirPort Base Station that has DHCP turned off, use the AirPort Admin Utility

[Quit]

10 Maintaining OS X

Despite its stability OS X still benefits from a robust maintenance regime. This chapter looks at some of the ways to keep OS X in top shape and also some general troubleshooting.

Time Machine

Time Machine is a feature of OS X that gives you great peace of mind. In conjunction with an external hard drive, it creates a backup of your whole system, including folders, files, programs and even the OS X operating system itself.

Once it has been set up, Time Machine takes a backup every hour and you can then go into Time Machine to restore any files that have been deleted or become corrupt.

Setting up Time Machine

To use Time Machine it has to first be set up. This involves attaching a hard drive to your Mac. To set up Time Machine:

Beware

Make sure that you have an external hard drive that is larger than the contents of your Mac. Otherwise Time Machine will not be able to back it all up.

1 Click on the Time Machine icon on the Dock or access it in the System Preferences

2 You will be prompted to set up Time Machine

A storage location for Time Machine backups isn't set up.
To choose a location for backups, set up Time Machine.

Cancel   Set Up Time Machine

3 Click on the Set Up Time Machine button

Set Up Time Machine

4 In the Time Machine System Preferences window, click on the Choose Backup Disk button

Choose Backup Disk...

5 Connect an external hard drive and select it

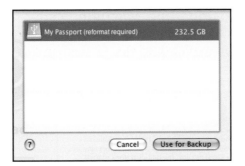

6 Click on the Use for Backup button

7 In the Time Machine System Preferences window, drag the button to the On position

8 The backup will begin. The initial backup copies your whole system and can take several hours. Subsequent hourly backups only look at items that have been changed since the previous backup

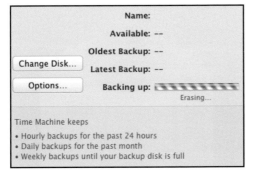

9 The progress of the backup is displayed in the System Preferences window and also here

Beware

When you first set up Time Machine it copies everything on your Mac. Depending on the type of connection you have for your external drive, this could take several hours, or even days. Because of this it is a good idea to have a hard drive with a Firewire connection to make it as fast as possible.

175

Don't forget

If you stop the initial backup before it has been completed Time Machine will remember where it has stopped and resume the backup from this point.

...cont'd

Using Time Machine

Once the Time Machine has been set up it can then be used to go back in time to view items in an earlier state. To do this:

1 Access an item on your Mac. In this example it is a document folder where the item Folder One has been deleted

2 Click on the Time Machine icon on the Dock

3 The Time Machine displays the current item in its current state. Earlier versions are stacked behind it

4 Click on the arrows to move through the open items or select a time or date from the scale to the right of the arrows

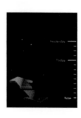

5 Another way to move through the Time Machine is to click on the pages behind the front one. This brings the selected item to the front. In this example Time Machine has gone back to a date when Folder One was still in place, i.e. before it was deleted

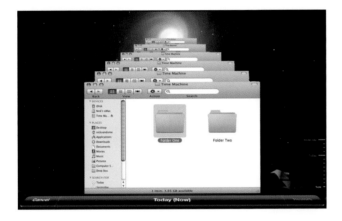

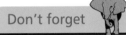

Items are restored from the Time Machine backup disk, i.e. the external hard drive.

6 Click on the Restore button to restore the item that has been deleted

7 Click on the Cancel button to return to your normal environment

8 The deleted item (Folder One) is now restored in its original format

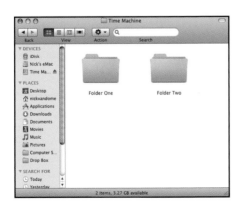

Disk Utility

Disk Utility is a utility program that allows you to perform certain testing and repair functions for OS X. It incorporates a variety of functions and it is a good option for general maintenance and if your computer is not running as it should.

Each of the functions within Disk Utility can be applied to specific drives and volumes. However, it is not possible to use the OS X start-up disk within Disk Utility as this will be in operation to run the program and Disk Utility cannot operate on a disk that has programs already running. To use Disk Utility:

Checking disks

Don't forget

Disk Utility is located within the Applications> Utilities folder.

Don't forget

If there is a problem with a disk and OS X can fix it, the Repair button will be available. Click on this to enable Disk Utility to repair the problem.

1 Click the First Aid tab to check a disk

2 Select a disk and select one of the first aid options

Erasing a disk
To erase all of the data on a disk or a volume:

1 Click on the Erase tab and select a disk or a volume

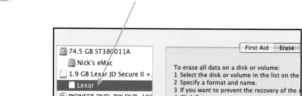

Beware

If you erase data from a removable disk, such as a pen drive, you will not be able to retrieve it.

2 Click Erase to erase the data on the selected disk or volume

Erase...

System Profiler

This can be used to view how the different hardware and software elements on your Mac are performing. To do this:

1 Open the Utilities folder and double-click on the System Profiler icon

2 Click on the Hardware link and click on an item of hardware

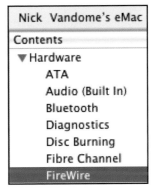

Nick Vandome's eMac

Contents
▼ Hardware
   ATA
   Audio (Built In)
   Bluetooth
   Diagnostics
   Disc Burning
   Fibre Channel
   FireWire

3 Details about the item of hardware, and its performance, are displayed

FireWire Bus:

Maximum Speed: Up to 400 Mb/sec

   iSight:

   Manufacturer: Apple Computer, Inc.
   Model: 0x8
   GUID: 0xA270004082B59
   Maximum Speed: Up to 400 Mb/sec
   Connection Speed: Up to 200 Mb/sec
   Sub-units:

4 Click on software items to view their details

iTunes	7.5
iWeb	2.0.2
Jar Launcher	12.0.0

iTunes:

Version: 7.5
Last Modified: 4/13/06 5:55 PM
Kind: Universal
Get Info String: iTunes 7.5, © 2000-2007 Apple Inc. All Rights Reserved.
Location: /Applications/iTunes.app

Activity Monitor

Activity Monitor is a utility program that can be used to view information about how much processing power and memory are being used to run programs. This can be useful to know if certain programs are running slowly or crashing frequently. To use Activity Monitor:

180

1 Click on the CPU tab to see how much processor memory is being used up

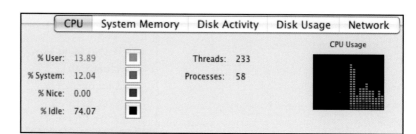

2 Click on the System Memory tab to see how much system memory (RAM) is being used up

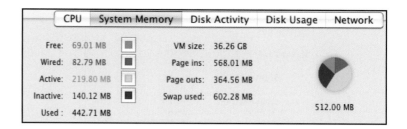

3 Click on the Disk Usage tab to see how much space has been taken up on the hard drive

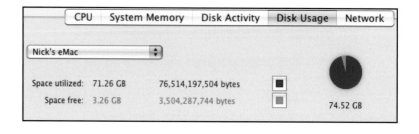

Updating software

Apple periodically releases updates for its software: both its programs and the OS X operating system. The latter are probably more important as they contain security fixes for the system that have come to light. To update software:

1 Click on the System Preferences icon on the Dock

Don't forget

In a lot of cases, software updates will be downloaded and installed automatically.

2 Click on the Software Update icon

3 Click on the Check Now button to view available updates

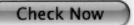

4 Check on the boxes next to the updates you want to install

Install	Name	Version	Size
☑	Pages Update	3.0.2	29.2 MB
☑	Numbers Update	1.0.2	27.4 MB
☑	iTunes	7.6.1	44.1 MB
☑	iWeb Update	2.0.3	18.4 MB
☑	iPhoto Update	7.1.2	15.9 MB
☐	Front Row Update	2.1.2	17.2 MB
☐	AirPort Utility	5.3.1	10.6 MB
☑	Mac OS X Update	10.5.2	341 MB

Don't forget

For some software updates, such as those to OS X itself, you may have to restart your computer for them to take effect.

5 Click on the Install button

6 Check on the Check for Updates box to have updates checked for automatically

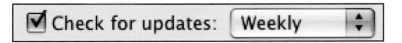

Restoring preferences

One factor that can cause problems with a program is if its Preferences folder becomes corrupted. This was a particular problem with OS 9 and earlier, but it can still occur with OS X. If a program is crashing a lot then you can try removing its Preferences folder and closing down the program. The next time it is opened, OS X will create a new Preferences folder that should be corruption free. To do this:

1 Click on the Finder icon on the Dock and click on your Home folder

2 Double-click on the Library folder

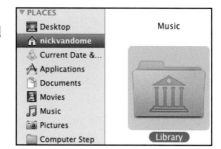

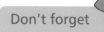

Don't forget

The problem of corrupted Preferences folders is a lot less common in OS X than in earlier versions of Mac operating systems.

3 Double-click on the Preferences folder

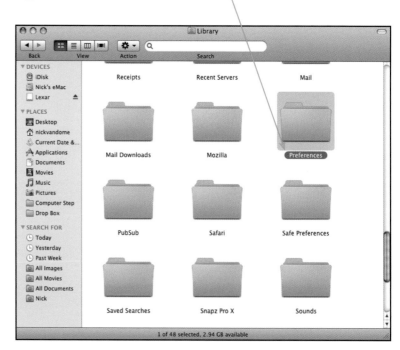

4 Select the Preferences folder of the program that is causing problems

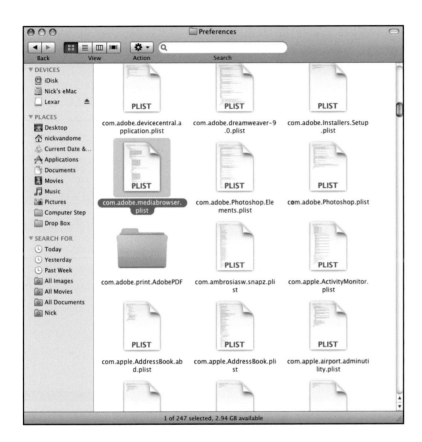

5 Drag the Preferences folder into the Trash. Close the program and then reboot

Problems with programs

The simple answer

OS X is something of a rarity in the world of computing software: it claims to be remarkably stable, and it is. However, this is not to say that things do not sometimes go wrong, although this is considerably less frequent than with older Mac operating systems. Sometimes this will be due to problems within particular programs and on occasions the problems may lie with OS X itself. If this does happen the first course of action is to close down OS X using the Apple menu>Shut Down command. Then restart the computer. If this does not work, or you cannot access the Shut Down command, try turning off the power to the computer and then starting up again.

Force quitting

If a particular program is not responding it can be closed down separately without the need to reboot the computer. To do this:

1   Select Apple menu>Force Quit from the Menu bar

2   Select the program you want to close

3   Click Force Quit

General troubleshooting

It is true that things do go wrong with OS X, although probably with less regularity than with some other operating systems. If something does go wrong, there are a number of items that you can check and also some steps you can take to ensure that you do not lose any important data if the worst case scenario occurs and your hard drive packs up completely.

- Backup. If everything does go wrong it is essential to take preventative action in the form of making sure that all of your data is backed up and saved. This can either be done with the Backup program available from the .Mac service or by backing up manually by copying data to a CD or DVD

- Reboot. One traditional reply by IT helpdesks is to reboot, i.e. turn off the computer and turn it back on again and hope that the problem has resolved itself. In a lot of cases this simple operation does the trick but it is not always a viable solution for major problems

- Check cables. If the problem appears to be with a network connection or an externally connected device, check that all cables are connected properly and have not worked loose. If possible, make sure that all cables are tucked away so that they cannot inadvertently be pulled out

- Check network settings. If your network or Internet connections are not working, check the network setting in System Preferences. Sometimes when you make a change to one item this can have an adverse effect on one of these settings. (If possible, lock the settings once you have applied them, by clicking on the padlock icon in the Network preferences window)

- Check for viruses. If your computer is infected with a virus this could effect the efficient running of the machine. Luckily this is less of a problem for Macs as virus writers tend to concentrate their efforts towards Windows-based machines. However, there are plenty of Mac viruses out there, so make sure your computer is protected by a program such as Norton AntiVirus which is available from www.symantec.com

Don't forget

In extreme cases, you will not be able to reboot your computer normally. If this happens, you will have to pull out the power cable and reattach it. You will then be able to reboot, although the computer may want to check its hard drive to make sure that everything is in working order.

...cont'd

- Check Start-up items. If you have set certain items to start automatically when your computer is turned on, this could cause certain conflicts within your machine. If this is the case, disable the items from launching during the booting up of the computer. This can be done within the Accounts preference of System Preferences by clicking on the Startup Items tab, selecting the relevant item and pressing the minus button

- Check permissions. If you, or other users, are having problems opening items this could be because of the permissions that are set. To check these, select the item in the Finder, click on the Actions button on the Finder toolbar and select Get Info. In the Ownership & Permissions section of the Info window you will be able to set the relevant permissions to allow other users, or yourself, to read, write or have no access

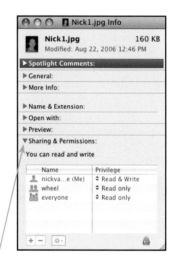

Click here to view permissions settings

- Eject external devices. Sometimes external devices, such as pen drives, can become temperamental and refuse to eject the disks within them, or even show up on the desktop or in the Finder. If this happens you can eject the disk by pressing the mouse button when the Mac chimes are heard during the booting up process

- Turn-off your screen saver. Screen savers can sometimes cause conflicts within your computer, particularly if they have been downloaded from an unreliable source. If this happens, change the screen saver within the Desktop & Screen Saver preference of the System Preferences or disable it altogether

Index